First Edition, University of the Trees Press, 1975
Second Edition, Planetary Publications, 1994

Published in the United States of America by:

Planetary Publications

P.O. Box 66 • Boulder Creek • California • 95006 • USA
800-372-3100 • 408-338-2161 • Fax 408-338-9861

Manufactured in the United States of America by BookCrafters
Cover Design by Sandy Royall
Cover Photography by JJ McCraty

Library of Congress Cataloging-in-Publication Data
Rozman, Deborah.
Meditating with children : the art of concentration and centering : a workbook on new educational methods using meditation / Deborah Rozman. - - Rev. ed.
p.   cm.
Includes bibliographical references.
ISBN 1-879052-24-5 : $14.95
1. Meditation for children.   I. Title.
BF723.M37R69   1994
158' . 12' 083—dc20   93-44420
                                            CIP

10 9 8 7 6 5 4 3 2

REVISED EDITION

MEDITATING
with
Children

the $\mathcal{A}rt$ *of*
Concentration
and
Centering

A Workbook on
New Educational Methods
Using Meditation

Deborah Rozman, Ph. D.

Planetary Publications
P.O Box 66, 14700 W. Park Ave.
Boulder Creek, California 95006

After receiving her doctorate in psychology, Deborah Rozman, Ph.D. founded a private elementary school and international teacher training center called Evergreen School which received much praise and acknowledgment. Since 1973 Dr. Rozman has taught transpersonal psychology, parent-child awareness groups, personal growth and development. She is the author of three children's tapes, three books and has edited numerous others.

Today, she is the Executive Director for the nonprofit educational and research corporation, Institute of HeartMath™, where she is busy developing programs for families, substance abuse counselors, educators and business professionals. Deborah has been on numerous radio and television shows, written many articles and was listed in *Who's Who in California*.

REVIEW EXCERPTS ON *MEDITATING WITH CHILDREN*

"Exceptional for guiding children to the meditation experience. Filled with practical exercises that children find fun and easy to do, the book is also one of the most direct introductions to meditation in print. Paradoxically, adults may find that they too get more out of this playful approach to meditation, in contrast to the forced discipline attitude that some schools foster. Written by an educator and psychologist, this book offers an exciting vision of our possible future. Do look for Rozman's other title *Meditation for Children*. These are quite possibly the best books in this exciting field."
— **MEDITATION MAGAZINE**

"*Meditating with Children* and *Meditation for Children* successfully integrate yoga, concentration, meditation, creative fantasy, movement, psychology and — most assuredly — love, in a way that clearly shows interested adults a path to fulfilling children's spiritual needs . . . many positive side effects occur . . . a heightened sense of community within the group, a sense of trust between adult and child, an ability to focus energy, greater creativity and a calm confidence are just some of the changes we've observed in the classroom."
— **NEW AGE JOURNAL**

"Meditation — not drugs — for the classroom."
— **SAN JOSE NEWS**

"Educators who once turned to Ritalin and other drugs for hyperactive children . . . are now turning to daily meditation exercises instead — with positive results."
— **SAN JOSE MERCURY**

TABLE OF CONTENTS

The Introduction

I wrote *Meditating With Children* in 1974 out of a recognition of the profound need among children to discover within themselves a deeper meaning to life. While there were many programs available to adults who were seeking to integrate their mental, emotional, physical and spiritual natures — through groups, teachers, books, churches, schools, courses of study, etc. — there wasn't and still isn't much that addresses this same need in children. Back in 1974, I saw children going through difficult upheavals as their parents' lives rapidly changed. These children were asking for help in many subtle and not so subtle ways. Increasingly, adults were going into therapy, either to recover from stressful childhood experiences or to unlearn poor attitudes and behaviors developed from childhood. But there wasn't much help for their children. I knew there had to be another way.

I had first learned how to meditate in 1970 and that opened a whole new world of discovery and deeper understanding of myself and others. Meditation gave me more ability to manage my attitudes and reactions to life and more awareness of my mental, emotional and physical energies. In college, I'd studied psychology and attitude change theory, but there were few techniques that brought the theories I learned into practice. Meditation, on the other hand, opened my heart and my mind to what inner peace and wisdom really could be. I so wished someone had taught me how to meditate as a child. It didn't make sense to me that children have to spend the first twenty years of their lives learning ineffective ways to deal with life and then have to spend the next twenty years trying to unlearn them if they ever do. It became my passion and my goal to find a fun, exciting way to bring the heart of the meditation experience to children.

Since the '70s, social change has accelerated at a tremendous rate. As a result, many parents, teachers and children struggle to find inner peace or a sense of security. Family, social and educational institutions have become unstable and precarious. Children today are more confused about values, have few modern heroes for role models and little certainty about their future. They turn on TV and see a steady stream of sex, drugs, violence and stress. The threat of youth gangs is rampant everywhere. Where is there hope for inner peace?

Trend analysis is showing that in the '90s more individuals and businesses are learning meditation techniques to reduce stress, improve health and find more peace. Meditation is no longer feared as religious but is considered a key to surviving the '90s and increasing the quality of life. But what about the children? They also need to learn how to find inner peace and security within their own hearts that is not dependent on people, places or situations. *Meditating With Children* was designed to do help them do that. Its purpose is to help adults teach children how to manage their energies to find inner peace, become heart-centered and discover the richness that lies within them. It is written as a workbook, to be used with children ages five through adolescence. Through fun meditations, activities and a variety of forms of creative self-expression, children begin to tap into their own inner resources. However, these techniques can be enjoyed by all of us "children" at any age. Since 1975, thousands of parents and teachers have told me how much they personally benefit from the meditations in the book. "If children can do it, so can I," is a common statement of many adults who bought the book just for themselves.

In days of old, prophets and seers taught in parables to convey depth of meaning to those who could understand their message no other way. The principles in this book are taught experientially through both objective, outer forms, and subjective, inner forms, so that the child experiences unity between the inner world of consciousness and the outer world of appearances and activity. In this way, a child can embark upon the integration of his or her total

Self. For example, we compare the way a walkie-talkie can be tuned to receive and transmit messages with the way our brains and hearts can be tuned to receive and transmit thought waves or feelings to each other. And, we compare the way a battery in an automobile works with the way our body battery works. By bringing energy consciously into the body through tensing muscles, and consciously releasing energy from the body by relaxing muscles, we observe the battery effect of charge and discharge that is going on continuously beyond conscious awareness. There are so many correspondences to be found between the world outside of our bodies and the world inside our bodies, that we study these facts of life and allow their truths to be revealed to us. Hidden in these experiences are keys to some of the mysteries of life and, most importantly, keys to better understanding the nature of our own Self.

HOW TO GET STARTED

While not a prerequisite, it is suggested that the leader of the group read through the entire book before leading the children through the meditations and exercises. The first part of this book provides the theoretical base from which the practical sessions presented in the second part were developed. Try to conduct sessions with small groups of children in similar age ranges. However, whether the size of your group is 1 child or 35, there are meditations and activities in this workbook that all can enjoy. They are structured so as to be adaptable to differing classroom needs and differing needs of families and teachers. Last but not least, it is suggested that parents and teachers participate in the meditations and energy activities found in the book with the children.

Over the years of using this workbook in public school classrooms, starting a children's school based on its principles, and continuing my own personal unfoldment, I've discovered new ways to make the meditations and exercises even more effective. In this new edition, all the meditations focus the children in their hearts — that place inside where we experience peace, fun, love and joy. The power of the heart enables children to release negative emotions more quickly, listen deeply to their own heart truth and appreciate and care more for themselves and others.

In my current position as Executive Director of the Institute of HeartMath® (IHM), a nonprofit research, education and training organization in Boulder Creek, California, I have been working with scientists, researchers, psychologists and educators in understanding the role of the head and the heart in the human system. Under the direction of IHM founder and president Doc Lew Childre, what we have discovered is that when the head (brain/mind) and heart (intuitive feelings) are out of phase, stress results, learning is inhibited, understanding blocked. Research at IHM laboratories shows that the heart plays a central role in the effective functioning of the brain, mind, emotions and immune system. Negative emotions tax the physical heart and the immune system, while positive heart-centered emotions, such as love, care, compassion and appreciation, create the opposite effect, increasing the efficiency of the physical heart, brain and immune system. This in turn accelerates learning. Doc Lew Childre's HeartMath system of personal, family and organizational empowerment teaches people of all ages how to use their heart smarts to unlock their inner potential for intuitive insight and creative problem-solving. *Teaching Children to Love* seminars for parents and educators and *Heart Smarts* seminars for teenagers provide children with reliable common-sense tools they need to listen to their hearts, activate intuition, build security within themselves and make responsible decisions. This truly is a next step for society.

The problems that plague the globe today are affecting *people*, and it is people who need new levels of care, cooperation and understanding. *Meditating With Children* is a start. It teaches children how to calm the mind and emotions and focus in the heart center where their innate core values of love, care and appreciation of life can be felt. The deeper that teachers, parents, and children, together, learn to find their real hearts and communicate from there, the more they increase their appreciation and understanding of each other. The result is a happier, more caring and productive learning environment.

Chapter 1

The Ideal

**Harmoniously balanced,
universally centered,
happy, calm, creative children.**

These class sessions will be an integrating factor in the lives of the children involved. A higher self-image is mirrored to them through the form, vibration and atmosphere of the class. Wholesome attitudes about life, human relations, use of energies, effective ways of expressing feelings about and with each other and working out differences – WHICH WORK TO FURTHER THE EVOLUTIONARY PROCESS – are the goals of each class period. With the prime objective of the classes being to instill a definite experience of unity and balance between the inner subjective worlds and outer objective worlds, the result will be an increased ability of each child to cope, to understand and to express.

In the classes we consciously link the inner and outer worlds through meditation, a going within and self-observation, discussing our understanding and expressing our awareness in activities. This process enables the children to develop a continuity of awareness between what goes on inside the body and what goes on outside the body. All activities are structured for the direct purpose of expressing and understanding the subjective self and for developing self-direction and self-realization in action. Through following the class formats given in the following chapters, the children's concentration, self-initiative, intuition, memory and imagination receive definite stimulation. By offering techniques to help children consciously become aware of being "whole" they are less likely to get caught in the traps of material identification and the problems caused by being embroiled in the glamours and illusions of people who do not know themselves and the world they have evolved. Being whole and unified we have defined as the experience of unity between that which lies within and that which lies without. This unity manifests as an ever-inclusive awareness of Self, revealing the nature of cause and effect as it activates energy in daily life. As much as possible the children are educated (the true meaning of education is "to lead out") to expand their awareness in terms of wholes, to identify and relate themselves through this unifying process to gradually revealed expanded patterns of Being and expanded states of awareness beyond the logical, linear and time-bound patterns presently imposed in education. Visual aids and the examples of great individuals whose awareness has transcended the normal mind patterns (the great scientists, poets, philosophers, mystics and saints) are particularly helpful tools for realizing these objectives. Children learn about essence through imaging, imitation and identifying.

In the new education, reading, math, physics and chemistry are explored in terms of causes and effects, and processes found in one subject can be related to another subject. Subjects as seemingly diverse as chemistry and drama are experimentally related in the class sessions. These correspondences can be noted as part of a new overall pattern of education, so that all the subjects studied become integrated as a Unity through understanding the rhythms and patterns that underlie them all. The consciousness of the child then becomes identified with these life-revealing patterns in an expanding dynamic awareness. The various subjects are realized to be part of an integrated Whole, rather than seen as separated, non-related, specialized fields of knowledge. The child then can come to terms with the whys and wherefores of what he is being taught in relationship to himself at the center and in context with his total life.

Two of the most essential areas of emphasis to achieve these presented objectives are the development of the faculty of CONCENTRATION and the faculty of the CREATIVE IMAGINATION. Both of these faculties are sorely neglected in present day education and bear discussion as keys to the new education.

CONCENTRATION

The ability to concentrate (or to focus the attention on any one thing for a duration of time) is directly proportional to the amount of true learning that takes place in an individual. By learning, we do not mean simply the acquiring of knowledge but the ability to penetrate deeply into the meaning underlying the knowledge being presented. Acquiring a high ability to concentrate endows the student with a corresponding ability to condense bodies of facts and information into a structural framework that reveals a deeper or more synthesized meaning than what is immediately apparent to the superficial or unconcentrated observer. The concentrated consciousness then acquires the potential for more rapid growth because of its ability to see meaning and to know the causes behind the appearances or the effects that continuously boggle the scattered consciousness.

The "boggling" is caused by the uncontrolled circulation of thoughts and impressions in the mind or the narrow-minded picking apart (and holding on to as reality) of certain aspects of these impressions. These activities of the mind are the norm and do not yield high level thinking and block higher intelligence. The discursive thinker does not have the ability or the power to develop the mind into an instrument that directly perceives the real behind the apparent until the necessary faculty of concentration is developed. It is the coherent concentration of mental and feeling energy that pierces the veil into the deeper levels of meaning to which all of the great scientists and philosophers testify. An attitude of concentration is emphasized throughout each class session and several exercises designed specifically to develop concentration are given.

IMAGINATION

The imagination or image-making faculty that all of us use continuously conditions our hopes and fears which condition our attitudes, which in turn condition our environment and what happens to us, which conditions our emotions and images again, in a never-ending sequence. When we begin to consciously become aware of the fact that we are continuously using the imagination to create our reality, we can begin to willfully create images of beauty, of harmony and of success by imagining them. When children are encouraged in their naturally active use of the imagination they can be taught to direct the image-making faculty to constructive purposes more easily than adults because they are less habit enslaved. They can be assisted to externalize their images in creative ways and, as the awareness develops, can begin to perceive the patterns and the effects that their use of imagination has caused.

Of course it is quite a step to go from the idea, vision or ideal to the real. To manifest the above objectives and goals requires steadiness of purpose, knowledge of method and perseverance in activity. Self-realization is an unfolding process and we must be prepared to exercise the needed patience along with the needed perseverance, especially since we, the teachers, are in the process of learning how it is done ourselves.

Chapter 2

Looking Ahead

**Educational methods
that teach children to truly
observe and listen from the heart.**

Education, like religion, is in the process of undergoing radical transformations to accommodate the growing recognition of the need to eliminate outworn forms that are no longer effective in providing for the optimal growth of children. New breakthroughs in science, in psychology, in self-awareness and in social awareness are bringing new light into the consciousness of man. This light will slowly lead to regeneration of our troubled educational system. As we find out more about ourselves and the universe in which we live, we know we must find constructive ways to share our new awareness with the next generation.

That traditional educational systems are no longer adequate for the growth of today's children is becoming increasingly apparent. One indication of the growing restlessness amongst many of today's young people is their voiced feeling that society in general doesn't care. Children become aware, as they grow older, of many inexplicable gaps that exist in life – gaps between what their parents say and what their parents do, gaps between their own inner life and their outer environment. With little or no opportunity to ever look at, confront and sort out these gaps, the child eventually becomes locked into them as the racial or social mode of existence or rebels from them, looking for escape. Because children do not know how to face these problems, they never really resolve them, even though some may be leading what society considers to be a normal life. Actually, most remain in the ambition and survival mode that these gaps create, cannot find their way out and are not fulfilled.

In light of this predicament it is evident that new educational methods should endeavor to discover what these gaps are and how to build bridges between them to illumine and resolve them. Eastern researchers, who for thousands of years have studied the nature of consciousness and how it works through humanity, have developed processes for building bridges in consciousness to close these gaps.* According to them, the prime functions for the educator in seeing that these bridges are built are:

1. To train the brains of children to respond intelligently to impressions coming via the senses. This is developed in the class sessions in this book through sense-awareness exercises.
2. To train the mind:
   a) To deal intelligently with information relayed by the brain (developed through aligning head and heart through directed use of energy in activity).
   b) To develop creative and imaginative thinking in response to physical impulses, emotional reactions and the mental world of the environment.
   c) To hear the promptings of the heart and unfold the spiritual self so it may emerge into active government through meditation and contemplation of life and nature.
3. To do this the educator must be capable of getting inside the world of the child and to help the child get inside the inner world of others. This can only be done through awareness of the heart.

Modes of accomplishing these objectives have been evolving in the West. The writings and works of Maria Montessori and Rudolf Steiner in particular

*Education in the New Age, Lucis Trust

10

have laid the foundation for new educational methods.

The practicum in this book is built upon the following guidelines:

For the first ten years of life the child is taught to truly observe and listen from the heart. When the heart listens, the mind hears. Young children are active and curious little beings. They are busy developing their senses. *Meditating with Children* teaches children to hear, see, feel, taste and touch with more awareness; they are given opportunities to respond to creative impulses through expressing creatively what they experience with their senses. The young child develops unconsciously through imitation, feeling and reacting to various stimuli. The arts, crafts, dramatics, music, all activities that give opportunity for creative response to stimuli, are helpful tools for growth and expression.

After age 10, the intellect begins to develop and this development is trained so that the child learns how to really discriminate in use of energy (which has normally been called learning right from wrong) so that emotions and desires can be better understood and managed. This is accomplished by comprehending how they work, what causes them, and what consequences they set in motion. A study of history, national laws, and their evolution, examination of social standards and values and their effects in relation to the child's own experience, are all excellent tools for teaching the above. Distinctions are drawn between memory training and thinking, between facts and their application to outward, objective events and their real subjective causes. A basic and operational understanding of the law of cause and effect as it operates in nature and in the subjective inner world of thought, feeling and attitude, and as it manifests in the child's external life, is cultivated through the study of science, of civilization and practical observation of the daily life patterns.

After age 17, an in depth study of psychology and the nature of the soul in relation to Life can be emphasized. While meditation will have been practiced from childhood, it will now be scientifically investigated and used by the student, based upon the premise that by this age the student has acquired a solid foundation of understanding the nature of cause and effect, natural law and love. As the heart-mind concentration develops, all deep thinking on any subject will utilize the faculty of the intuition, as well as the intellect.

Of course the effectiveness of this type of new education depends upon the faculties and abilities of the teachers involved. An understanding of character traits of the children in relation to modern psychology, modern medicine, spiritual and vocational disposition will lead to greater and more individualized child guidance. The goal of the educational process will be the unification of the subjective and objective worlds, the inner and outer life, so that the child functions as an integrated Being and the life of the higher self can begin to manifest.

The 20th Century has often been called the atomic age, and more recently an age of increased social or group awareness. The dynamic potential of group awareness can be conjectured to be as great as the potential of the fusion of nuclear or atomic energy. This group awareness is not to be confused with the herd instinct, rather it develops through the deep recognition on the part of individuals of the essential Oneness of Life. Through the fostering of an awareness of the universality of life processes and through a loving, unifying environment, self-consciousness becomes transformed into group consciousness and can then make contact with its nuclear Being. The individual looks forward to good for others as much as for himself because he increasingly

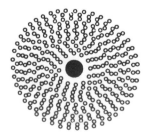
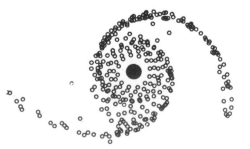

experiences no separation between himself and his fellow man. Love and awareness of life process dissolve the barriers. Identification with the whole develops. When this identification and love occurs within members of a group, true fusion based upon a realized at-one-ment takes place in the group awareness creating the same dynamic energy potential as that of nuclear fusion at the atomic level.

The process of education begins with teaching the child to teach himself. This is carried out by the child being led into the position of inward search by the teacher. The child is asked Why? Why ask this question? Why is nature thus? The responsibility for answering questions is thrown upon the child as much as possible yet the teacher will still drop suggestions when necessary into the mind of the child to encourage him. The purpose of this method is to have the child learn to draw upon his own authority, not to look for or demand an outer reply which can be memorized. She will learn to think and intuit for herself and draw her own conclusions. In effect, the child will be taught to condition his own life. Through learning the process of thinking in the heart and careful observation the child learns to discriminate and contemplate conditioning energies in his environment as different energies in action and not to see them so much as events or circumstances that are to be accepted or rejected due to emotional reactions of like and dislike. "As a man thinketh in his heart, so is he."

It is only through practical trial and experiment that these goals will be reached, not through theoretical discussion and continuation of the old ways of teaching. This is not to suggest that the old methods be overthrown, but that they be supplemented with new methods, so that in due time the old methods will be outgrown.

The central purpose of this book is to offer practical methods to actually introduce new light into the life of the children of today – into their hearts, their homes, their after school classes, and into the schoolroom itself. We have immediately before us the opportunity and the privilege to cultivate a new being, a new generation, a new type of child in our civilization. There are certain prerequisites to any type of cultivation. One prerequisite is the environmental condition. To grow this new type of child the atmosphere of the environmental setting must be one of love, where the child realizes he has no cause to be afraid or shy, where he is treated courteously and is expected to treat others similarly. An atmosphere of patience, without the sense of pressure, fosters a balanced and rhythmic growth. An atmosphere of honesty and understanding cultivates honesty and understanding in the nature of the child. Growth and still more growth is the emphasis, but it is an organic growth process, based upon expanding awareness. The child is encouraged to express and is listened to and assisted in developing self-motivated activity. The child is helped to develop the attitude that apparent barriers or obstacles to progress are only challenges for greater growth and opportunity, so that she can cease identifying with any limiting condition and can begin thinking in terms of expanded possibilities for herself, for the group, and later for the world in which she lives.

Children come to the world endowed with an open heart and certain natural abilities to perceive clearly which become clouded as interaction with the external environment (home, school, society) increases. By keeping the heart perception open the child is able to perceive life's experiences clearly and to extract the wisdom and the needed lessons from them without delay.

The enlightened vision of the future as it becomes merged into the present will reveal to mankind all the tools that are needed to begin to truly optimize the process and the progress of an individual's evolution.

"Truly I say to you, Except ye become as little children you will never enter the kingdom of heaven. . ."

Chapter 3

Discipline

**Teaching through the
heart generates and sustains
constructive and positive attitudes.**

It is important that discipline be kept in the class sessions so that the true meaning of listening, of observing, and concentrating can be understood. The greater the concentration the greater the benefit that will be received from the classes. It is an essential part of the class to have the leader remain centered in the heart, calm yet firm. The children respond more to the leader, teacher or parent's attitude than to anything else. Teaching children should basically be done through the heart center to generate a secure, sustaining aura of enveloping love. The *reason* for any discipline that is imposed should be clearly conveyed so that it is received harmlessly by the child, in order to cultivate harmlessness in the children.

When children direct negative energy to each other or to the leader, the leader endeavors to non-verbally transmute the energy within himself and then send it back through the heart and mind as positive love, while simultaneously endeavoring to verbally resolve the difficulty. As this method is practiced it becomes apparent that verbal communication will not always be necessary the non-verbal exchange of energy becomes sufficient to get the message through and create the desired attitudes. This technique enables the teacher to maintain control over the group through direction of energy, which works to keep the class coordinated and unified. The teacher disciplines himself to think only constructive and positive thoughts and therefore harmless thoughts about the children. When frustration does occur for the teacher it should be processed through the heart and shared honestly and forthrightly with the children to maintain an atmosphere of open honesty. It is also necessary for the teacher to keep in tune with the needs of the children both as a group and individually. Too much restlessness may indicate a need to modify the session to more activity. If one child is a disturbance she will disturb the energy equilibrium of the entire group and must be redirected to other activities outside of the room where the group is meditating. She can be told that she may return when she is ready to get back in her heart and cooperate.

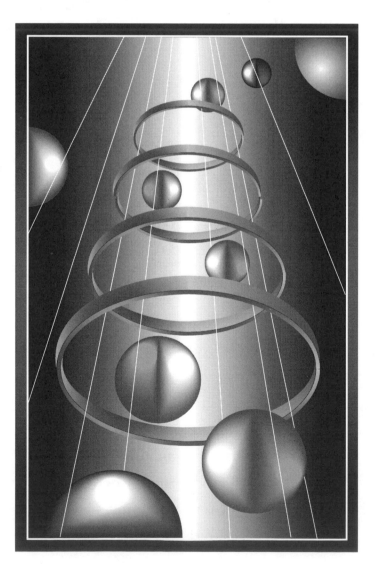

Chapter 4

Class Structure

**Structure and function,
form and rhythm duplicate
natural, universal patterns.**

The exercises, meditations and activities which make up what we call a session or class are structured in a pattern for specific reasons. The Universe appears to function in rhythmic patterns. Duality can be seen manifested everywhere. Day and night, life and death, the in and out movement of the ocean tides are evidence of this duality. Duality can be seen as the very heartbeat of the universe. Just as we recognize two basic movements in our own heartbeat, the diastole and systole, so there are two basic energies often called positive and negative, throughout the manifested world. As we observe the universe we can also see structure and function, form and rhythm within that form. We attempt to duplicate these natural, universal patterns in the class sessions.

The human body can be seen as a microcosmic expression of a macrocosmic system. There are patterns of duality observable in the universe that are observable as well within the human mechanism. The human lungs draw energy into the body and let energy out of the body via air by means of the breath. The lungs keep the heart pumping blood into the entire body and back again into the heart with steady rhythmic order. We attempt to externalize this basic, natural pattern in the classroom by consciously drawing energy from the body into the Source of Life and Consciousness in the heart and receiving regenerated energy from this Source through meditation. We alternate meditation (consciously directing the attention and energy inward to the heart) and activity (consciously directing the attention and energy outward) and replicate thereby the diastole and systole of the macrocosm. Each activity is followed by the meditative process called *centering* and each meditation is followed by the active process which *grounds* the energy. Practiced over a lengthy period of time, it can become a foundation of balanced living for the child throughout life. It is not expected that the child will consciously grasp the implications of the patterning. However, it will dawn on her consciousness as it becomes a part of her, and as she observes the lives of others in relation to her own.

CENTERING MEDITATIONS

These are done often, in between periods of activity, are kept short and are lengthened only as depth is attained. The objective is to establish a true recognition of Center within and the purpose of centering so as to tap into the Source of Security, Consciousness and Life for more Peace, Joy, Inspiration and Fun. It is important that the first meditation of each class period be fun. The purpose of this is to reach a unified group energy and create a positive experience.

If it is necessary to ask the children to sit a little longer to establish a sense of GROUP Peace and GROUP Balance, then do so, for Balance and Peace are essential for an effective session. Proceed very slowly with building the length

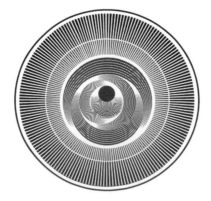

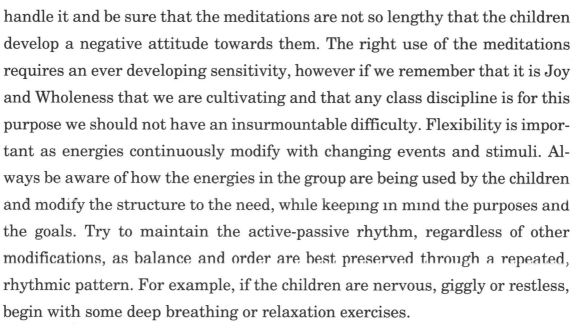

and energy level of the meditations. If the teacher stays calm in the heart, she or he will be able to trust intuition for the right duration of the meditation process. Be sure the energy level does not exceed the ability of the teacher and of the children to handle it and be sure that the meditations are not so lengthy that the children develop a negative attitude towards them. The right use of the meditations requires an ever developing sensitivity, however if we remember that it is Joy and Wholeness that we are cultivating and that any class discipline is for this purpose we should not have an insurmountable difficulty. Flexibility is important as energies continuously modify with changing events and stimuli. Always be aware of how the energies in the group are being used by the children and modify the structure to the need, while keeping in mind the purposes and the goals. Try to maintain the active-passive rhythm, regardless of other modifications, as balance and order are best preserved through a repeated, rhythmic pattern. For example, if the children are nervous, giggly or restless, begin with some deep breathing or relaxation exercises.

It is always good to have on occasion a group discussion session during which children have an opportunity to discuss their feelings. Too often this is overlooked totally in public schools, until some point of real distress or crisis is reached. Such a class period can include discussion by older children on the nature of emotion as energy in motion. They can be encouraged to discuss their own energies-in-motion and help each other to realize the true causes. With older children the investigation can take them to the understanding of feelings as the cause of emotion, and certain thoughts, ideas or basic attitudes as the cause of many feelings. This tracing down process can help with an understanding of our relationships with others. It can also reveal causes and effects which we are usually unaware of, leading to true contemplation of motive. The result is improved use of energy. With younger children (under 10) it is more effective to deal with emotions when they happen (as an illustrative example) or in heart talks, psychodrama, gestalt, or redirection into energy release activities rather than rationalizing or theorizing. Younger children do not have the mental development for the first type of discussion. With all age groups it is important to create opportunities for feelings to be openly shared and expressed in beneficial ways.

TIPS ON CLASSES

The teacher should be in equilibrium before the class commences. Meditation for equilibrium and a humble inner request for guidance from the Higher Self, the Source within the heart, sets the tone, not only for the teacher, but for the children as well, for it must be remembered that children respond to the vibrations of the teacher.

Moods can be created in the environment to calm the children, such as restful music, incense (the odor can carry a soothing vibration), and candlelight. If appropriate, children can be asked to take their shoes off when they enter the group circle. The circular position is recommended as a means of sealing the group energy and focusing it into the center. Since a circle represents a continuity, the energies may have less of a tendency to get distracted. All of these suggestions may be experimented with for optimal tone setting.

- Have one good, deep meditation each session.
- Have one project that is explored in depth. The class will evolve in direct relationship to the depth of the experiences both in the meditation and in the activity.
- Have the children lead the meditations occasionally, allow them to choose the meditation format.
- Have 2 reserve or alternate projects that can be used in case a

change of course is needed in any session. Always have your structure for the session prepared, however alternatives may be needed and when they are planned for there need be little or no break in continuity of the group energies.

• It is important to maintain spontaneity in order to avoid rigidity and optimize creativity. Here again a balance between the form and the rhythm is essential.

It is always smoother, but not always possible, to have the meditations on tape* or memorized or totally spontaneous, so the teacher participates and experiences with the children. The voice should be smooth, calm and relaxing. Sometimes, and especially with younger children, it may be necessary to monitor the class during the meditation so a few disruptive children do not spoil the silence for the others. The earlier the tone is set that *no* distractions will be permitted during the meditation period, the easier it will be and the better the growth and progress of the group.

Be sure the children are seated far enough apart so that no one is touching. Have them sit in a comfortable position (cross-legged on the floor or sitting in a chair with feet flat on the floor) with the back straight. Explain to them that a straight back allows the energy to flow freely up and down the spine which helps meditation. Have them place their hands on their thighs palms up to receive and balance the energy. It may take quite a bit of reminding before the habit of a proper meditational posture is learned and becomes automatic. However, this discipline in the formative years will help to prevent sloppiness in the later years. If a child finds it is just too uncomfortable to continue to stay sitting upright, he may quietly lie down on his back without disturbing the others and continue the meditation lying down.

* *Meditating with Children* meditations are available on cassette from Planetary Publications.

The Class Sessions

The Class Sessions

Each of the following class outlines is accompanied by a worksheet on the right-hand page. The worksheet is just as important a part of the growth experience as the meditations and other awareness expanding activities. On it are listed self-study questions for the leader, questions that may be put to the children to stimulate creative thinking, and space – for notes. Many times spontaneous inspiration of new ideas for creative changes and improvement will come and it's important to jot these impressions down as soon as they are received or they will be gone forever, as evanescent as a dream.

The worksheet can also serve as a record of your progress with the different exercises and meditations. Listen to your heart. Write down your feelings as well as your thoughts.

Activities experienced through the heart can take you to even deeper, richer feelings.

General Class Outline

These class methods can be applied to any time schedule alternating from 1/2 hour to a full school day using the basic rhythm of centering then activity, and modifying this outline to fill the need.

1. Leader meditates before class if possible to receive guidance from the Source within for the class session and to set a tone of peace and love within herself or himself and within the class-room. Radiate your heart energy to the children as they enter and during the class. Love is a powerful tonic. Sending heart will help you and the children feel regenerated and have more peace and fun.

2. Children enter and take off shoes for greater relaxation and less restriction (not always feasible to take shoes off, so create through some method a relaxed environment).

3. Initial short discussion of whatever children want to share to empty the mind and feelings.

4. Tension and relaxation exercises (these are introduced in detail in the beginning class) or yoga postures (see back of book).

* 5. Quieting the breath, observing the breath in meditation posture: sit up straight as if you are a puppet being gently pulled up straight by a string that's stretched from the middle of your head. Sit cross-legged with the back and neck straight and the hands upturned on thighs, palms open. Breathe in slowly to the count of 5,

* **See page 98 for more on conscious breathing.**

General Class Outline

hold to the count of 5, breathe out to the count of 5. Repeat 3x, or more.

6. Go into the meditation and make sure the energy reaches a harmonious level so that this initial meditation of the class session reaches the needed depth to set a good vibration in motion for the rest of the session. Insist on calmness and a good meditation. The meditation can be previously planned by the leader or spontaneous depending upon the teacher's class plan and the teacher's intuition of the need of the moment.

7. Discuss the meditation experience or lead the children directly and consciously into directing their calm energies into a project. A project that has some correspondence to the subject of the meditation period is preferable.

8. Discuss project.

9. Clean up.

10. Consciously bring the energies back together again within by going into meditation.

11. Have an active game after meditation if the project was fairly passive, or passive game or activity (e.g. story) if project was an active one. Occasionally a snack can be substituted for a second activity if the first activity was long.

12. Love Circle (introduced in the beginning class).

All of the following meditations and activities can be interchanged, after being done as written one time, for varying effects and to adapt to varying needs. The age of the children, the nature of the group, are variables to be considered when planning classes.

General Class Outline Worksheets

1. Was I calm and centered before the children arrived?

2. Did I really succeed in drawing the children out so that real feelings were expressed? How could I have done better, and what changes will I make next time?

3. How are we going to achieve quiet so that no one is disturbing? What should we do?

General Class Outline Worksheets

4. Did I prepare the projects well or did the energy get scattered?

5. Was a good tone, a good vibration present in the group throughout?

Your Ideas

Beginning Class

1. Leader meditates before class to set an atmosphere of peace and love (amazing the effect this has on kids).

2. Children come together and sit in a circle on the floor or in chairs.

3. Leader begins by asking children what meditation is, what energy is? What are some examples of energy? What does it do? Where does it come from? Where does our energy come from? Get the children really discussing between themselves. Discuss meditation as a means of relaxing and withdrawing into our Source within to receive a fresh supply of energy and awareness from that Source. We do this each time we breathe, each time our heart beats, and now we are going to do it consciously, throughout our whole Being through meditation.

4. First we all stand up so we are not touching. And we are going to first practice sending energy into our arms and withdrawing energy from our arms by tensing our arms so that they vibrate with energy and now relaxing our arms and letting all the energy out. Now let's do the same thing with our legs and now with our whole body. Now let's do the same with our body again only this time we breathe in the energy as we tense the body so it vibrates with energy and then we breathe out as we release the energy and relax . . . and again let's breathe in and tense and vibrate our bodies, just like a guitar string vibrates when you add energy to it by plucking it with your fingers, now let's breathe out and relax as we release the energy from our muscles.

5. Now let us sit down again in a circle, cross-legged, no one touching or talking. We sit up straight but relaxed so energy from the Source within can flow up and down our spine into our brain. Let's put our hands on the place where our legs meet the rest of the body and turn the palms up so energy can flow through our hands.

Beginning Class Worksheet

1. Did we as a group gain any new understanding about energy?

2. Were the children quiet enough to really experience the meditation?

3. Ask the children to give examples of opposites to help them understand the in and out rhythm of the sessions.

Your Ideas

Beginning Class

6. Now close the eyes and listen . . . very carefully to your breathing, in and out, listen to it slow down. Now put your attention on your heart and listen to it beating inside you. Now breathe in slowly through your nose, keeping your mouth closed as I count to 5. Now hold to 5 (count 1 - 5). Now breathe out through your nose very slowly (count 1 - 5). Repeat 5 times. Now, while keeping your eyes closed look inside your heart, that place inside where you feel love and care or cared for. Focus at that spot. That place is one of the doors into the Center of your being, the Source from where your awareness and understanding come to you. Now concentrate on the Source at that spot by putting everything you feel or think right there and see if you can feel a quiet peace, deeper than when you sleep at night . . . stay there with it, be still . . . . Now, come out of the Source, slowly, come back into your heart and open your eyes.

7. What did you feel or notice in your visit to your Source within? Have each child share his experience. What did you see, etc.? Accept whatever the child says whether you think it is fantasy or not. The fantasies can be the first steps to the real. If the child didn't feel anything, it's okay. If the child felt sad feelings, ask everyone to send love and heart energy to the child. Ask the child to send love to those feelings. Love helps everything.

8. Discuss the effect that meditation will bring, the purposes and goals outlined in this book. Adapt the discussion to the age group. Talk about how love is an energy that makes us feel good.

9. Have a stopwatch or use a large clock and see how long each child can concentrate from the heart before shifting attention. Introduce the purpose and meaning of developing concentration to the children – to understand themselves, other people and the meaning of things more deeply.

Beginning Class

10. Do a quiet project such as art, etc., with the children. Remind them to watch how the energy is working through them as they create, so they can be aware of the energy inside themselves as it moves from the Source within through their hands onto the paper.

11. Clean up the project.

12. Sit in a circle to bring the energy back into the Source and be reenergized again before the next activity, so that with each activity we have a fresh supply of energy and consciousness that we have consciously tapped from the Source within. Lead the children through the meditation process again. This time let's dip into the Source in our heart like we are dipping a pail into a well and drawing forth the energy as if we were drawing forth water and pouring that energy from the Source all through our body to reenergize it. Feel recharged by all this new energy.

13. Discuss rhythm in nature and the rhythm of the classes which will be centering-activity-centering-activity to withdraw energy into the Source and direct it out and withdraw it in and again direct it out, just as we tensed and relaxed to recharge our bodies earlier. Just as the heart beats in and out and the breath goes in and out. Just as the sun comes up when it rises and there is light during the day, and goes down when it sets and the light is withdrawn and disappears into darkness.

14. Have a fun game with a lot of motion action.

15. End with a love circle. Everyone standing up and holding hands. We all send love to each other as thanks for sharing in the Source together.

**Child's Drawing
from
Meditation**

Beginning Class Worksheet

1. Did the children get a beginning grasp of what peace in the heart is all about?

2. Did the children feel loved, cared for and supported?

3. Have a chart for each child to record his own progress with heart concentration.

4. Was the energy built up during the meditation time well-directed into the activities?

Your Ideas _____

Second Class

1. Do steps 1 through 5 in the basic outline on page 26.

2. Do one of the imaginative meditations where the children use visualization, e.g. the plant meditation on page 86.

3. Discuss the nature of channeling energy as briefly outlined in number 28 on page 113.

4. First begin by channeling energy from the right hand to the left hand of your own body and see if you can experience any sensation. Use your imagination to feel the energy flowing in the top of the head, through your heart and out your hands.

5. Then everyone channel love and light to each other's heart center one at a time, so each person has a chance to directly experience the love in the center of the heart. When the hand gets tired — switch to the other one – keep the attention going so everyone gets the same energy. (Good for concentration.)

Second Class Worksheet

1. Did a soothing, good feeling come over everyone as a result of all the channeling?

2. Did I remind the children enough to stay concentrated and to use the heart and imagination to keep the energy flowing?

3. Did everybody feel connected in a new way to plants or animals?

Your Ideas _____

Second Class

6. Share experiences.

7. Channel love to plants, fish, etc. Relate this channeling of love to the sun that shines its light on all of us every day, sustaining us with the love of its light. And each of us has a source of light, a sun within us that sends light and love to those we direct it to.

8. Discuss animals the children love and feel close to.

9. Meditate again on the sun or Source within and send light and love from that sun to someone you feel who needs it, who would be happier because of it just as the love and light you felt in your heart today made you happier (perhaps a parent, grandparent, friend, etc.).

10. Have a snack or activity, such as music and movement to music feeling the energy flow and pass through you.

11. Love circle to thank each other for sharing in the Source.

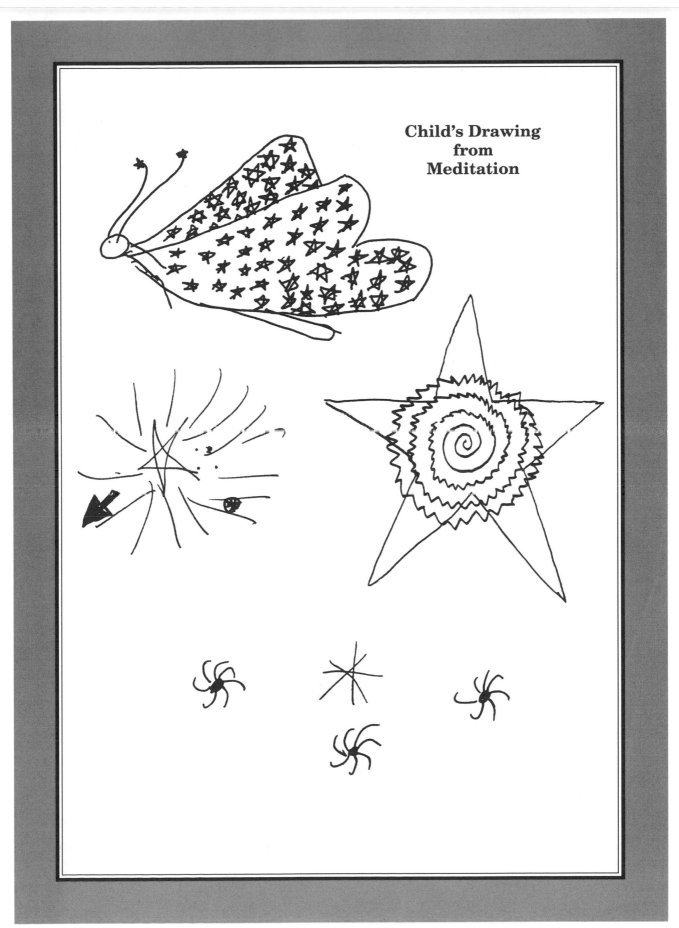

Child's Drawing from Meditation

Third Class

1. Do steps 1 through 5 in the basic outline on page 26.

2. Do meditation number 4 on page 70.

3. Review what has been accomplished in the first 2 sessions, asking the children what each has liked the best so far.

4. Do a science experiment – 7 on page 105. Discuss how meditation enables us to draw in more energy from the Source and to build up our ability to be a brighter light, have stronger hearts, increase our intelligence, be more loving and more powerful or effective, just as when we turned up the amount of energy going into the light bulb it became brighter and more powerful because it could light up a greater area. Bring in a 3-way bulb to demonstrate. How do our tension and relaxation exercises do the same thing for our bodies? Develop the analogies and ask the children questions, stimulate their intelligence and confidence to be bright and shining lights.

5. Meditate and go into the Source within the heart and in that One Source feel that you are One with everyone else's Light, Intelligence, Love and Power. Be very still and listen – within – look – within. Sing a tone softly to fill the whole circle and the whole room with your experience of the Source within. (See exercise 38 on page 117.)

6. Have you ever hummed or sung along to the vacuum cleaner at home? It's fun and makes you vibrate with sound energy.

7. Use the charts of evolution and of the brain in the back of the book, or develop one of your own that you prefer. Discuss the growth of intelligence

Third Class

in the mineral-plant-animal-human-superhuman-Infinite.

8. Go outside and find examples of the 3 kingdoms, mineral (rocks), vegetable (plant or flower), and animal (snail, worm, etc.). Put them in a box, one group at a time. Meditate on each kingdom – concentrate on each from the heart and try to get inside of it. Feel what it's like to be a rock, or a flower or a snail. Are you heavy? Afraid? Observe how the Source works energy through them in different ways. Pose questions to the children.

9. Short meditation – spontaneous, led by the leader. Be inspired by the vibration that has been created thus far by the class session.

10. Snack or short, simple activity.

11. Love circle to thank each other for sharing in the Source.

**Teacher's Drawing
from
Meditation**

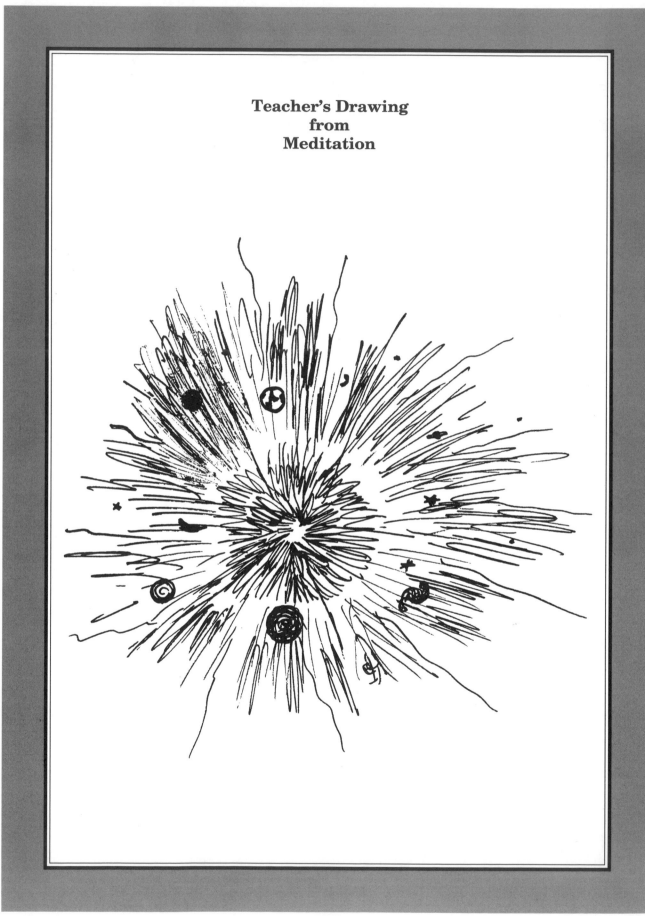

Third Class Worksheet

1. Did we feel the different worlds inside a rock, a plant and an animal?

2. Do we have an understanding of evolution of intelligence from the charts?

3. Is the Love circle becoming a meaningful quiet sharing?

Your Ideas _____

Fourth Class

1. Do steps 1 through 5 in outline on page 26. Introduce a few of the yoga exercises in back of book.

2. Do meditation number 8 on page 80.

3. What is peace? Ask children.

4. Read the story on page 146, "Where is the Source?"

5. Discuss how we too can experience the Source of Love in our hearts but we must learn how to be very quiet and still, both inside and in our bodies, so that we can see and hear what is deep within us and not what is going on outside of us, so we can find out who we really are. We must shut out all noisy sounds and listen to the sounds inside. We shut out all the sights by closing our eyes to see the sun within. We keep our body still because when we move it attracts our attention and we feel different things but we want to feel the peace and love in the center within instead. So let's send heart energy to someone we love and make our love grow bigger. We send love and care out from our hearts and know that the more love we send out, then the more love we can feel inside.

6. Do experiment number 9 on page 106.

7. Meditate on this heart stillness by stopping all the ripples of the body and the mind and just loving.

8. Draw what the Source means to you (or paint).

9. Love circle (as previously given).

Fourth Class Worksheet

1. Are the children beginning to experience the reason for inner peace and even enjoy it?

2. Have I used relaxation methods to prepare the children for meditation, if they have been restless?

3. Can I present incentives to help them go deeper?

Your Ideas _____

Fifth Class

1. Do steps 1 through 5 in the basic outline on page 26. Introduce the rest of the yoga exercises in the back of the book.

2. Do meditation number 1 on page 64.

3. Discuss what colors we saw inside. Discuss our favorite colors. Beautiful feelings and thoughts create beautiful colors. Hateful and mean feelings and thoughts create muddy or ugly colors. Use a prism and discuss the spectrum, the rainbow, the rainbow of colors inside us that the sun or Source inside us creates, just like the sun outside us creates the rainbow after the rain.

4. Paint pictures using the 7 colors of the rainbow or just the colors you saw in meditation. Mix the primary colors to get other colors.

5. Clean up.

6. Meditate: Sing a tone (exercise number 38 on page 117) and order the body to be still. Sing a tone and order the feelings inside to be still. Meditate on the stillness that this sound brings, keeping concentrated on the stillness, keeping everything under orders to be still until the leader sings . . . and then we all sing to vibrate energy back into the minds, and sing sending energy back into the feelings and sing to vibrate energy back into the body. (Sing tones loud, medium, whisper and mentally.)

7. Snack or other activity.

8. Love circle.

Fifth Class Worksheet

1. Are the exercises and postures developing more aware-ness of how energy works in our bodies?

2. Do we sometimes sing to the vacuum cleaner? a droning engine? other sounds? Do we feel the energy in the sound?

3. Encourage the children to practice meditation at other times to center themselves. Ask them what it is doing for them. Do they sometimes center before they go to sleep? Or when sad or upset?

Your Ideas _____

Sixth Class

1. Do steps 1 through 5 in the basic outline on page 26 or yoga exercises.

2. Do meditation number 2 on page 66.

3. Discuss past week awareness. Name and share important feelings that you experienced. Discuss some of the particular problems that we may have experienced. Have the children help each other by going to their hearts to come up with solutions to the problems.

4. Do the Gestalt technique with one or a few of the problems by putting the problem or the person causing the problem in one chair (through the imagination) while the child experiencing the problem sits in another chair facing the first chair. Have the child talk to the problem or person in the other chair telling from his heart what he feels and what his experience is. Then have the child switch chairs and sit where the imaginary problem or person was sitting and become that problem or person and tell the child who he has left (himself-who is still sitting in the second chair) what the problem or the person feels about the child. Continue the dialogue back and forth helping the child to see from the other point of view until a heart understanding is reached on the part of the child.

5. Do a creative drama exercise depending on the age of the children. Plan this out before the class session.

6. Have a child lead the next meditation.

7. Snack or other activity.

8. Love circle.

Sixth Class Worksheet

1. Are feelings a touchy subject? How can caring for each other help us to have the trust to share more deeply and help each other?

2. Am I unsure about sharing my inner world with others?

3. Are we gaining a closer family feeling through these sessions? If not, how can I help this to happen?

Your Ideas _____

Seventh Class

1. Do steps 1 through 5 of the basic outline on page 26. Add to this outline a new energization exercise. Make fists with your hands and gently tap your fists all over your head. Concentrate your attention between your eyebrows and command your sleeping brain cells to wake up.

2. Meditate to a tape of uplifting music. Focus on the music with your heart as you listen.*

3. Discuss the earth as a school and the fact that according to science people are only using 1/10th of their brain cells. Show the chart of the brain in the back of the book. What goes on in the other 90% of the brain cells, what potentials are waiting there like a seed to sprout? What abilities will we develop? Ask the children – what's a miracle? Discuss miracles from history. Relate miracles to the development of inner abilities due to the waking up of some of the brain cells. Discuss channeling which seems like a miracle because it is new to most people and exercises brain cells that most people aren't aware of.

4. Do the water witching game number 18 on page 109.

5. Discuss.

6. Leader guides a meditation.

7. Snack or activity.

8. Love circle. Send the greatest miracle of love to any unhappy or sick person you know. Thank each other for sharing in the Source and in the Love.

* *Heart Zones*, excellent music for meditation, is available from Planetary Publications

Seventh Class Worksheet

1. Are we making a chart of our concentration ability?

2. Have we been increasing our length?

3. Have results of better concentration shown yet in other activities?

Your Ideas _____

Eighth Class

1. Do steps 1 through 5 of the basic outline on page 26 plus the new exercise given in the seventh session. Do this new exercise from now on along with the others.

2. Do meditation number 10 on page 84.

3. Five Senses – what are they – see number 11 on page 106 and number 31 on page 115. The real you is not just your body, your senses, your feelings which come from your senses, your thoughts which also come from your senses and feelings. The real you is beyond the senses and is really One with the Source. Learn to be the real You, and use your thoughts and feelings and body as tools to learn and grow and play with just as you use a pencil as a tool to write with, a paint brush as a tool to draw with and a hammer as a tool to build with. In everything – remember you are the Love, the Light and the energy in the Source and everything else is your tool to learn and to express that Source. Ask the children, how do we use our tools of the body? of feelings? of thoughts?

4. Do 5 projects, one with each sense emphasized, e.g. looking at pictures, listening to music, smelling flowers or perfumes, touching water and stones and cotton (items of different texture), tasting different spices, etc. Discuss.

5. Meditate on going beyond the senses to our Source in the heart center within, so we can learn to do it quickly.

6. Love circle.

Eighth Class Worksheet

1. Have I been able to really forget myself and merge into the meditations, or am I always worrying about the class or something else?

2. Can I see how the 5 senses are limiting and also how we need to become more sensitive?

3. Am I growing and changing with the kids?

Your Ideas (and feelings) _____

Ninth Class

1. Do steps 1 through 5 of the basic outline on page 26 or yoga exercises.

2. Do meditation number 7 on page 76.

3. Do experiment number 19 on page 109 and 30 on page 115.

4. Do wheel meditation, number 6, on page 74.

5. Choose one of the more active activities and do.

6. Love circle.

Ninth Class Worksheet

1. Have I ever had a telepathic experience?

2. Ask the children if they can remember any telepathy with friends or family, e.g. knowing the phone was going to ring 5 minutes before it did, knowing exactly what someone was going to say before they said it. Share examples.

3. Have I ever thought through how sound goes from mouth through the microphone onto a tape? How is it similar to the way we create mental tapes that we play over and over in our heads?

Your Ideas

Tenth Class

1. Do steps 1 through 5 of the basic outline on page 26 or yoga exercises.

2. Do meditation number 5 on page 72.

3. Discuss astronomy, the solar system, the sun and the planets and then relate to the 12 signs of the zodiac with simple, fun astrology. Have each child write down his name and sun sign on a separate slip of paper. Have the children of the same sign sit next to each other and then the same elements, fire, earth, water, air, sit together. Experiment with observing each sign walk around the room, naturally. See if we can see any similarities. Does he seem fiery when he walks? Does he move fast? Does he move slow and ploddingly with his head down? Does he move lightly? Does she seem earthy? Does she seem watery? (This exercise and others can let the children explore for themselves the attributes of astrology. It worked well with the first group the author worked with and not at all well with the others, due to the many variables in astrology. Practice and have fun! This exercise does not always yield results correspondent to the sun sign of the child. However, it is a good exercise on observation and can be fun.)

4. Meditate on your sun sign. Ask yourself what it means to you.

5. Write a creative story on the meaning of your sun sign to you. Have very young children draw pictures on what it means to them.

6. Do a short meditation on going into the Source where we are not any sign, where we are all One.

7. Snack or activity.

8. Love circle.

Tenth Class Worksheet

1. Can I actually accept the idea that the whole universe is experienced in my consciousness?

2. Ask the children if they were able to expand their mind-balloon to include everything in it. Is there anything left out? As soon as you name something you've included it in your awareness.

Your Ideas _____

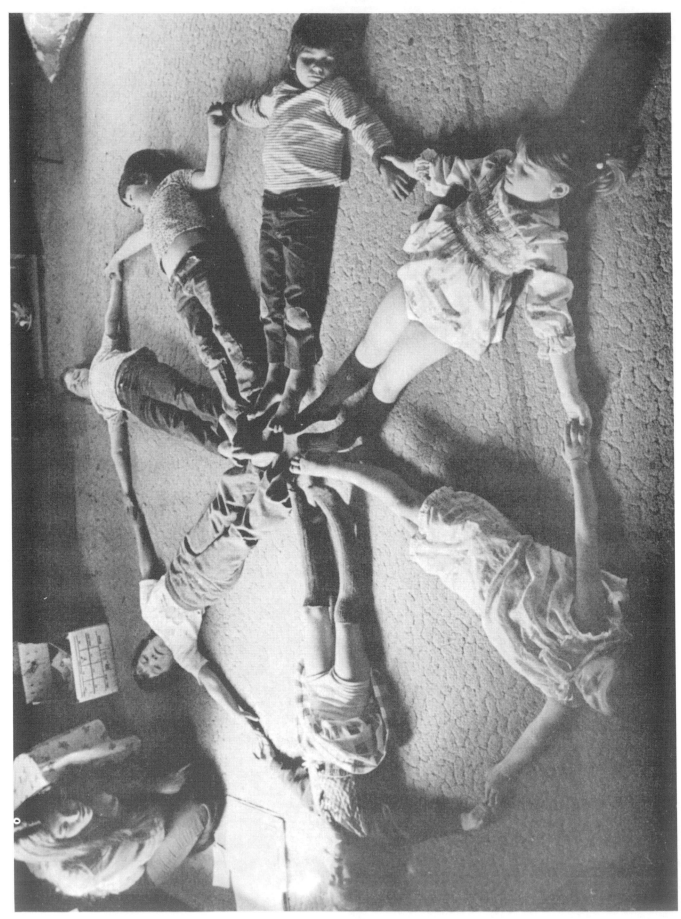

The Meditations

The Meditations

The following meditations are integrated into the class sessions. They can also be done by the children at any time. They are not only exercises in creative imagery, but have planted within them seeds which can awaken new realizations about life.

As you read them aloud feel the inherent rhythm. Each meditation must be read, like a poem, with varying intonation and musical sensitivity in order to convey its message. Tune into your center, then into the children and then into the meditation to discover how it can best be communicated. Whether you memorize the meditations, put them on tape or read them from the book directly to the children, tune into your listeners so you know when to pause and when to speak. The . . . markings mean pause, but some situations may need more or fewer pauses – rely on your intuition.

Growth and awareness through attunement to the heart intuition.

These sample meditations should give the leader or parent or teacher a good foundation to build on. The classes are to be an opportunity for growth and creativity for the leader as well as the children. So the leader should use these sample meditations and sample class outlines as a means to structure the classes and avoid some of the difficulties that would occur if there were no guidelines. The teacher, however, should look to his or her own intuition and spontaneous inspiration to add to them and to bring the NOW into the class experience.

The growth of awareness is important for the leader as well as for the children. Once the attunement with the basic rhythm and structure has taken place, modifications, improvisations and whatever else that works to foster the achievement of a more integrated child and group can be added. With the spiraling developments in methods and techniques for creative growth being presented throughout the world, the leader should have no problem in keeping the program of self-discovery going and growing, using the basic format and information outlined here as a guide.

Again worksheet space is provided for your own comments and creative ideas.

The eyes should always be closed throughout the meditation until the leader says to open them at the end.

**Child's Drawing
from
Meditation**

1. The Circle and Dot Meditation

We all sit very still and make sure no one is touching . . . That's the way. In your heart see a dot with a circle, and you are the dot and the circle is the world around you. See what color your dot is and see what color your circle is. (GO VERY SLOWLY, WHILE STAYING ATTUNED TO THE ATTENTION SPAN OF THE GROUP) . . . very still . . . very quiet . . . Now, put Love in your dot with you; and as you love your dot gets bigger, and the more you love with your heart, the bigger the dot . . . the more you love the bigger the dot . . . and it gets bigger and bigger and bigger (still quiet) and bigger and bigger until all of a sudden the dot and the circle are one. Oh . . . and what color is your dot? and what color is your circle? . . . and now what color did it all become? The more love, the bigger it got. Did you know that the circle is really many more dots just like yours? (This meditation is especially good for very young children. Discuss what they saw afterwards.)

1. Worksheet

1. Did your dot grow to include the whole world? Can you imagine the whole world inside of you?

2. Let's all be dots and imagine we are growing so big that all the stars are inside of us, all the grass, trees, oceans and people and sky. What does it feel like?

Your Ideas

2. All Is Energy Meditation

Be very still and quiet. Make sure no one is touching. Feel your toes; now feel them disappear into light. Now feel your feet. Feel them disappear into light. No feet, only light. Feel your ankles and feel them disappear into light. Feel your legs and feel them disappear into light. Feel your knees and feel them disappear into light. Feel your buttocks and feel them disappear into light. Feel your stomach and feel it disappear into light. Feel your chest and feel it disappear into light. Feel your arms . . . feel them disappear into light. Feel your shoulders and feel them disappear into light. Feel your chin and feel it vanish – disappear into light. Feel your mouth and cheeks and nose dissolve and disappear into light. Feel your eyes and forehead dissolve and disappear into light. Feel the top of your head disappear into light and now feel your whole head disappear into light. Now there is no body, it has entirely disappeared into light. Go deep inside the real you, that is beyond your body.

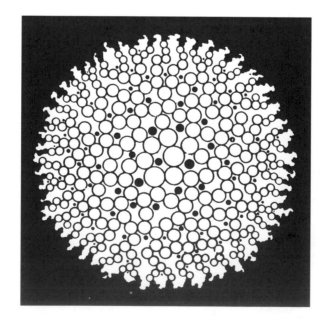

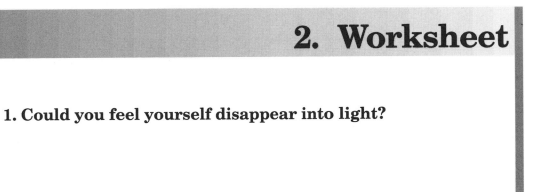

2. Worksheet

1. Could you feel yourself disappear into light?

2. Did you really forget your body and feel the real you that is not your body?

Your Ideas _____

3. Spaceship Meditation

Imagine there is a spaceship inside of your head. Step inside your spaceship. Now, go all the way up in your spaceship, out of the top of your head past billions of stars, up, up, up, up . . . . . (pause) . . . observe what you see, now go all the way down in your spaceship . . . down, down, down, down, ... (pause) . . . now go all the way up, up, up, up higher and farther this time . . . . . now go all the way to the left . . . . . farther and farther, now go all the way to the right . . . . . farther and farther and farther, ... now all the way straight in front of you, farther, farther, farther, farther, ... (pause) . . . now all the way behind, go farther and farther back, on and on, farther and farther . . . . . (long pause). Now, come back slowly to the center and back into the top of your head and now you are inside your head again. You have traveled over and through the entire universe. Open your eyes, look around you. What did you see in your universe? Discuss with each other. (Adapt this meditation to visit a star, a planet, the center of the sun, etc.)

3. Worksheet

1. What did you see in your universe?

2. Did you visit the Milky Way?

3. Did you feel the heat of the sun?

Your Ideas _____

4. White Light Meditation

This meditation is especially good to do anytime we are afraid. The white light will wash the fear away and it can also be called a protection meditation which we do to protect ourselves from unpleasant feelings, nightmares or mean people.

Imagine a waterfall of white light about 3 inches above your head and feel it flowing into the top of your head and through your whole body. Feel its water pouring into your face and neck . . . Feel the white light water gushing into your arms and chest and heart . . . feel it pouring down through your stomach and legs and feet until your whole body becomes part of the waterfall of white light . . . Now see this light whirling inside, feel it coming into your very consciousness and holding your attention so you become ONE with it.

4. Worksheet

1. **Did we properly relax and concentrate before beginning the meditation?**

2. **Did the light wash away any unpleasant feelings we may have had?**

3. **Have I ever had reason to use this meditation to wash away fear?**

Your Feelings _____

5. Balloon Meditation

Feel a balloon inside your heart. Now we are going to blow up our balloons. But these balloons are very special. They never burst, they just keep expanding and expanding and expanding. Feel your balloon expand, blow it up in your imagination a little bigger, and bigger, and bigger, feel it getting so big that it is bigger than your whole body and is expanding everywhere . . . Feel it bigger than this room, feel it bigger than the city, bigger than the country, bigger than the oceans, bigger than the whole world . . . (long pause) . . . now blow it up once more so that it is bigger than the whole universe and all the stars and the planets and the sun are inside your balloon too, and imagine that every idea and every thought and every feeling is inside the balloon.

5. Worksheet

1. Did I read this meditation slowly enough so that each expansion took us deeper and farther into our Self?

2. What color was each one's balloon?

3. Could everyone really feel everything inside of them?

Your Thoughts

6. The Wheel Meditation

Everybody lie down on the floor with their feet touching each others' feet in the center of the circle which is the hub of the wheel. The heads are the rim of the wheel at the outside of the circle and the rest of the bodies are the spokes of the wheel. Now, close your eyes, hold hands with the person on your right and on your left. Now imagine yourself moving, imagine in your heart the whole wheel moving around and around to the left. Now feel it moving the other way, around and around to the right. Feel it moving as the heart of the whole universe. Your wheel is the heart of the universe, the rhythmic wheel, the pulse-beat that keeps the world in motion. All the stars and galaxies are moving in your wheel. See them spinning in your mind's eye. Feel you are a part of everything, of everyone, everywhere . . . . . . Now, relax and melt and be.

6. Worksheet

1. Did we feel our Self going round and round spinning first one way, then the other?

2. Then did we finally melt into the stillness, into the silence where there is not motion?

3. Could we feel oneness with everyone experiencing the same thing?

4. Young children often want to act out the images, move their hands and bodies. You can encourage this by having them stand in a circle and physically move as well as move in their imaginations. They can spin around the wheel like whirling dervishes (in an orderly manner) and then gently fall to the floor, lie down on their backs and close their eyes. If they have trouble keeping their eyes closed, it's because they are not relaxed enough. Speak in a soothing voice and ask them to pretend there is a heavy weight on each eyelid keeping it closed. Then read the meditation to them again while they are still, and ask them to move only in their imaginations. This helps integrate the physical and imaginative development, and the same sequence can be done with other meditations.

7. The Temple Of Light Meditation

Sitting very quietly and straight, we are going to build a temple of Light. Imagine a golden thread of light coming out of your heart and going into the heart of the person next to you in the circle on your left . . . Now imagine another golden thread of light coming out of your heart and going into the heart of the next person on your left. Now imagine another golden thread of light coming out of your heart and going into the heart of the next person (repeat this until everyone is connected with everyone and the circle is complete).

Now, still very quietly, imagine a thread of blue light going from your spiritual eye (right between your eyebrows) to the spiritual eye of the person on your left. Now imagine another blue thread of light going from your spiritual eye to the spiritual eye of the next person on your left (repeat until everyone is connected with everyone else's spiritual eye and that circle is complete).

Now, imagine a thread of white light going from the top of your head, the crown, to the crown of the person on your left. Now imagine another thread of white light going from the top of your crown to the crown of the next person on the left (repeat as before until the circle is complete and everyone is linked with everyone else at the crown with white light).

Now we are all linked up with everyone and let us feel that our Temple of Light is built and let us send love down the threads we have built into each other . . . . . . Now let us softly sing OMMMMMMMM, and send the sound down the threads of light we have built, first down our golden threads from our hearts, then down our blue threads from our spiritual eyes, and now down our

76

The Temple Of Light Meditation

white threads from our crowns. Feel the love, the peace, the bliss we have in our Temple of Light. Now let us feel thankful inside to the Source within that has given us this beautiful family experience with each other.

(This exercise can be done in the opposite direction as well, proceeding from right to left. Visual aids are helpful, such as the string pictures on black velvet-like backgrounds that are available in crafts stores. These show what a network of colored strings looks like in different geometric patterns.)

7. Worksheet

1. Did I, as a leader, maintain one-pointed concentration while guiding the children through this meditation?

2. Were we all attentive to the flows of energy we were sending and receiving?

3. Did we feel a presence of some special energy that embraced us all together?

Your Feelings

8. An Outdoor Meditation

To be done very slowly. Sitting very quietly with eyes closed, imagine a star twinkling in your heart. Imagine its rays of energy streaming from the star radiating light. This light is lighting up whatever it falls upon just like the sun lights up the earth with its rays. Whatever you put your attention to, there you will be directing that stream of light . . . Now open your eyes and look at a blade of grass. See the light from your star light up the grass from within the grass, from the inside of the grass revealing the grass to your eyes. The light which you direct is lighting up the light in the grass showing the grass to you. The light is your spirit, the light is the spirit of the grass, one light, one energy of life. Look around you and see the spirit of everything as light, see the light of life, everywhere . . . light, energy, life.

8. Worksheet

1. This exercise can be done on a tree, an animal, a rock, a cloud, another person – anything.

2. Did anyone feel like they experienced their own consciousness creating the grass?

3. Where is the grass experienced?

4. Where is the sun experienced? Why?

Your Creativity _____

9. Gravitation and Radiation Meditation

Concentrate on the core of your heart – that place where you have felt loved and cared for. Bring all your energy in your whole body to that point. Draw it up from your toes and feet and legs, now up your spine into the center of your heart. Draw the energy down from your head, throat and shoulders into your heart. So we draw all the energy together in that one point, like gravity bringing it all in. We concentrate it there.

Then we expand that point and our energy expands too. We begin to radiate out like rays from the center of the sun. We feel that radiation energy expand out through our body, beyond our head, beyond our mind, into the entire room, filling it up with our awareness. Now feel your awareness expand right through the walls of the room, right through the atoms and molecules that make up the walls, into the yard, the whole block . . . the grass and trees . . . down into the earth. Now expand your awareness to include the sky and beyond into space – out into the sun and all the stars and planets. Feel it expanding beyond all the stars, beyond the beyond . . . radiating. Now forget yourself and just Be.

9. Worksheet

1. What does gravity feel like?

2. What does radiation feel like?

3. What is the difference between gravity and radiation?

Your Thoughts _____

10. The Five Senses Meditation

Go into the Source within. Quietly, let's draw all the energy out of our body into the heart center, the sun within. Now let's make sure our eyes are closed. (Blindfolds can be used for younger children to take away the temptation of peeking and to make the meditation deeper). Pretend you have never seen anything before, that you were born blind and have never seen color or other people or anything . . . what's it like? . . . Now imagine that besides being blind you have never felt or touched anything before, that all your feeling is in the center within and you've never touched your body or the floor or walls or your mom. How do you know anything is out there? How do you know there is space if you can't feel? . . . Now let's take away our hearing. Imagine that you can't hear anything. Bring all the sounds outside or inside your head back into the Source within . . . now, very still, imagine you can't smell anything . . . You have never smelled any food or any flowers. All you have left is taste . . . Now let's take the taste away. You've never tasted anything. All your senses have disappeared into the Source. What's left? . . . Now disappear your very self into the Source . . .

As we come back let's add the senses one by one. First let's taste the taste of our mouth, then smell the air . . . Now listen very carefully. What sounds do you hear in the distance? . . . Now move the body, feel the space, feel the floor, pinch yourself . . . Finally let's open the eyes and look around at the colors.

10. Worksheet

1. Do I now realize I am not just my senses and my body, but something else?

2. Could I really experience how no sense of touch means no objects and no space?

3. Were my senses sharper when I came back to them?

Your Ideas _____

11. Plant Meditation

Sitting very still with eyes closed, or open and focused on the plant, imagine that you are floating out of your heart center into the leaf of the plant.

Feel its flatness, its leafiness, its greenness; now imagine that you are floating down the stem of the leaf into the big stem that carries food and energy to all of the leaves: watch the liquid rising up the stalk and as you go down the big stem see the tiny little cells that make up the plant.

Now, go down farther into the roots under the dirt. Feel the roots drinking the water and absorbing the minerals from the dirt to help keep the plant healthy and growing. Now, go back up the root into the stalk and into one of the tiny little cells in the stalk and be that cell.

Now, go inside the Source of life within the cell which is the same Source of life inside you, and feel the oneness of the Source of all life everywhere. Now come out of the stalk and out of the plant and back to your heart.

11. Worksheet

Do with plant experiment on page 110.

1. Could we distinguish between the air moving the plant leaf and the vibrations of energy coming through our hand moving it?

2. Was the plant more responsive to some people than to others?

3. Could we feel like we were talking plant language?

4. Were we able to forget ourself and become the plant? How did it feel?

Your Impressions _____

Elements: Fire Meditation

1. Do 1 through 5 in the basic outline on page 26 or yoga exercises.

2. Discuss: What is fire? How do we use it? Where do we find fire? candle? fireplace? sun? stars? What does fire provide? heat? energy? light, etc.? We want to experience the nature of fire today.

3. Have a candle lit and have each child one at a time and then together concentrate on the candle flame, just on the flame, and go deep inside of it and become one with it. Time the duration of the child's concentration. Discuss the importance of concentration. Have the children all look at the candle together (which is in the center of the circle) and then close their eyes and concentrate on the reflection of the candle flame inside their inner eye.

4. Fire meditation. See a flame, like the flame on a candle, inside your head. It is yellow with blue inside the yellow and white inside the blue just like a candle flame. Feel it get warmer and warmer – feel it spreading – now step inside the flame and know that you are a glowing light. Feel yourself glowing – first yellow – now feel the heaviness of the body and the feelings and the mind burn away in the yellow flame leaving you free. Now go deeper into the blue of the flame. Feel the blue as love, as joy. Now go deeper still, into the white until you see, and now feel and know yourself to be standing inside the white center of light of the flame which is very hot and very cold at the same time. Meditate on that.

5. Did anyone have trouble keeping their attention on the candle flame inside their head and going deep into it?

6. Make candles as a project with the children.

7. Snack or quiet activity.

8. Love circle.

All these element meditations are fun to do on a day when the moon (and if possible sun) is in the sign of the particular element.

Fire Meditation Worksheet

1. Was I able to go beyond the idea that fire burns and experience its energy inside myself?

2. Did we experience the calming effect of flame?

3. Did anyone see colors flashing in the background or see energy waves?

Your Ideas _____

Elements: Earth Meditation

1. Do steps 1 through 5 in the basic outline on page 26 or yoga exercises.

2. Earth meditation. Imagine you are the earth, one with Mother Earth. Feel that you are deep inside the center of the earth and that the mountains and oceans and rivers are your body. Feel all of the rocks as part of you, now feel all of the soil and dirt as part of you, . . . now feel all of the little plants as part of you and all of the big trees as part of your body and the grass is like your hair, . . . now feel all of the animals as part of you, . . . and now feel all of the people, everywhere, black and white and red and yellow, as part of your body. Feel all of the earth beings as part of you, the earth, whom you feed and shelter and give a home to, for all have the same home, the earth.

3. Discuss the earth – what does it mean to you?

4. Discuss ecology and nature's cycles.

5. Discuss earth as a school again as a review or if not done before introduce it for the first time. See chart at back of the book.

6. Make something out of clay.

7. Meditate, feel that all of the things that live on earth are here to learn and when they finish learning on the school of earth they will enter into the One Source which is beyond the earth but which is always with them when they are on the earth too. And they will continue learning beyond what we can even imagine. Let us go deep inside our Source.

8. Love circle.

90

Earth Meditation Worksheet

1. **Am I able to see our meditation-activity routine as an ecological cycle?**

2. **Are we really communing with Mother Earth, feeling her solidity and her nurturing?**

3. **Ask the children if they find it is easier now to feel what others are feeling and in general have a deeper understanding of others. Has meditation changed any of our relationships?**

Your Ideas _____

Elements: Water Meditation

1. Do steps 1 through 5 in the basic outline on page 26 or yoga exercises.

2. Water meditation. Close your eyes and feel that you are in an ocean of blue light; feel and believe that you are a wave in that ocean and are floating up and down, gently up and down just like a wave. Now feel yourself melt and disappear into that ocean just like the wave disappears into the ocean, ahhh, feel it relaxing you. You are now one with the ocean of blue light and there is no wave, no difference between you and the ocean. Now listen . . . very quietly within . . . hear the sound of the ocean inside your head, and feel yourself becoming one with that sound. Now the sound is dying away and the wave is starting to come back again just like the wave in the ocean comes back after it has disappeared and forms into another wave and another and another until it washes into the shore and we open our eyes.

3. Do finger painting and movement to music, being waves in the ocean.

4. Meditate on the ocean again, feeling the ocean containing all people, all life inside of itself, go deep into the Source as the ocean of all life, the ocean of all energy.

5. Using a fish bowl, observe how the fish swim in water and are always in the water; they were born in water and die in water and because they are never out of water they do not know that they are in water – they don't know anything that isn't water. To them everything is water and nothing is water. Similarly, we live in a sea of energy that we don't recognize is energy because we are born in it and live in it and die in it and don't know anything that isn't it. Discuss.

6. Snack

7. Love circle.

Water Meditation Worksheet

1. Did I read the meditation slowly and rhythmically so the children could follow along?

2. Did we all really get into the essence of ocean-ness?

3. To feel the nature of water more we can listen to rain, water coming from the faucet or trickling over stones in a brook. Try to feel it. Meditate on and become a rain drop.

Your Ideas _____

Elements: Air Meditation

1. Do steps 1 through 5 in the basic outline on page 26 or yoga exercises.

2. Air meditation. Close your eyes and feel the air around your face and around you whole body. Feel the air as it comes inside your nose as you breathe in and as it leaves your nose as you breathe out. Air is everywhere and it is breathing you in and out, in and out. Listen to the sounds that travel to you through the air. Open your eyes and see the light of different objects around you that travel to your eyes through the air. Air is everywhere. Birds fly through air. Air fills all space. Close your eyes and see the space inside yourself. Meditate on the space and let it get bigger and bigger until you know that the space of the whole universe is inside of you.

3. Fly kites with the children or do some other project that involves air.

4. Meditate on air. Close your eyes and in your imagination pretend you are flying through air and are going anywhere that you want to go, way up over the oceans and the mountains into space, beyond the sun, beyond the stars, beyond the beyond . . . now you are coming back into the universe, you are flying back, passing the stars, passing the sun, and coming in to earth, and passing over the ocean and the mountains and into the class and into your body and here you are.

5. Telephone, television, telegraph, radio, tape recording, walkie talkies, etc., all provide examples of vibrations moving through air. Play with one of these to demonstrate. Have a musical instrument, e.g. guitar, and illustrate how the sound moves through the air from the instrument to your ears.

6. Snack or activity.

7. Love circle.

94

Air Meditation Worksheet

1. Did we gain some understanding about sound waves traveling through air? light waves? thought waves?

2. How is it that our imagination can travel through all of space to any part of the universe?

3. How is it that we can look out at the stars at night and travel in our minds way out beyond them? Where does our consciousness stop?

Your Ideas _____

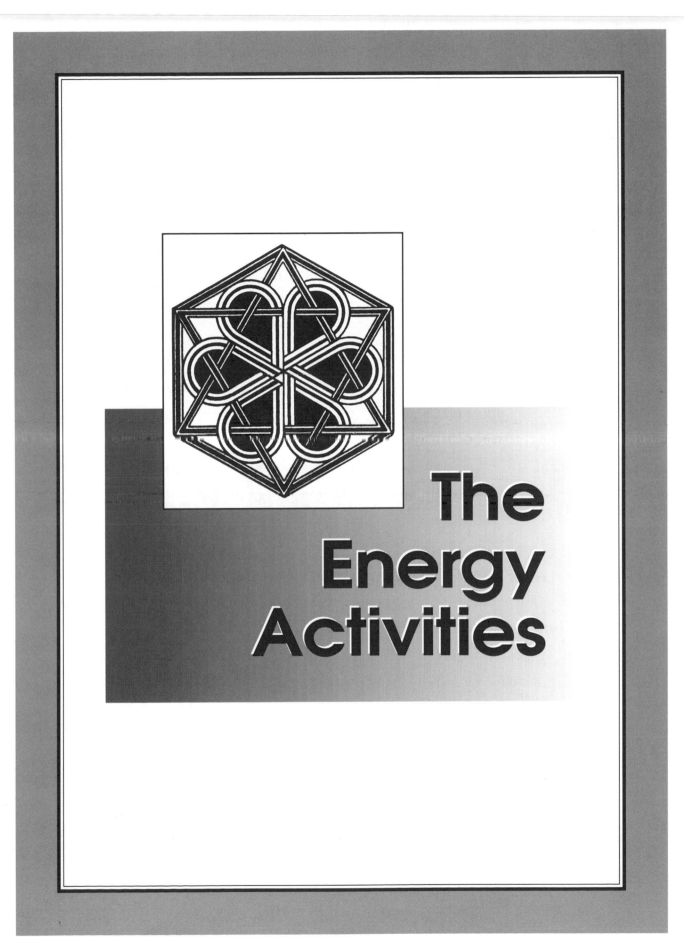

The Energy Activities

The Breath

We have discussed breathing a little in the class sessions. The rhythm and direction of breath can be a complete study in itself. When we use our imaginations in rhythm with breathing, we energize whatever image we have in mind.

To help get in touch with the pent-up feelings, relax your body from the toes to the scalp, letting go of each body part as you travel up the body, first one foot then the other and so on. Now, it's time to use the breath. Breathe in deeply through the nostrils, focus in your heart center, and ask yourself, "What am I feeling? Do I still have some old hurts from someone who was angry with me? What memories come to my mind? Did someone ignore me whom I wanted to feel love from? Is there someone I have funny feelings about?"

Breath can be directed to help us get in touch with these inner feelings and clean out negative emotions or pent-up resistance. Breathe in and release the pain or hurt with each breath. The breath technique will not solve your problems, as you must get to the cause of the disturbance in order to find the solution, but it can release the negative feelings and effects the problem has on the nervous system. With each breath you remember to hold a new image in your heart to take the place of the old feeling you have gotten in touch with. That new image might be love, peace, sending nice feelings to another, feeling like you are floating on the ocean, or whatever comes to mind to make you feel calm and peaceful. The power of your imagination creates your feelings, happy or sad, and you can use that power to change your feelings. It is important to charge up the new image with life force from the breath.

The Breath

Get in touch with the hidden feelings. Relax. Take a deep breath of fresh air, feel whatever is there, put in the new image and then let the feeling go as you breathe it out. Breathe in again, image, wash the feeling from your heart, breathe out and release it, let go. Feel fresh life force fill you up with a clean, new feeling, nicer than before. No matter what another person has done to you, you do not have to let it pull you out of your heart center with bad feelings. Send some of your fresh life force on a wave of love to someone who has disturbed you. They may be disturbed too! Now when you are centered you can go to the person you felt funny towards and talk to him or her about your feeling. Find out what this person really feels about you. It might be different than what you are thinking.

Breathe in as you bring your life energy within and breathe out as you send your life energy out into the world around you. Let your self expand and fill the whole of space.

You can practice these breathing exercises while you are walking, running, playing, exercising or being still. Before bed or after an argument are especially good times to get in touch with feelings and release them.

Energy Awareness Projects

When introducing new concepts and words to children it is important to do so in terms of the children's own experience. For example, ask them: What are some examples of energy? or Can you act out (or mime) what energy means to you? Instead of lecturing the child we draw out the answer from the child.

Depth of concentrated study will depend upon the age of the children. Don't feel defeated if you, as the leader, know little or nothing yourself about these different processes. Do some research with basic science texts to precede these activities. A brief understanding is all that is required to draw the basic analogies. With older children you can embark on research projects of any or all of these areas together, sharing with each other the information and discoveries, relating them to the meditations and to daily life as much as possible.

JOURNAL KEEPING

After the meditation write down or draw your thoughts and experiences. Expand on them to include your feelings about life, your relationships with family and friends. Daily journal keeping helps us clear our feelings and understand our self better.

Concentration Exercises

1. Use a candle flame and practice concentrating on it. Feel like you're sitting inside it, becoming one with it. Feel you are the whole group sitting inside the candle flame. Time the length you can do this without moving.

2. Concentrate on pictures of energy diagrams (see mandala on page 141). Look for colors, spinning light, petals going to the right and to the left.

3. Concentrate on the second hand of a large clock when working as a group or use a watch, when working individually. Make a chart for each child to note improvement daily.

CONCENTRATION FOR DEEP RELAXATION

Sa Ha Breathing — Watch the breath as if you are watching someone else breathe. Watch it go in and out and in and out. Watch the rhythm. As breath comes in, mentally say the word Sa to yourself. As the breath goes out, mentally say the word Ha. Sa, Ha. Don't force the breath, let it flow. This simple exercise is the foundation of many popular types of meditation and relaxation. It can be done from 1 to 20 minutes. If there is trouble sleeping at night the Sa Ha breathing can correct it.

Energy Awareness Exercises

1. After the initial coming together in a circle, have the children sit in different geometric shapes for their meditation, e.g. a triangle, a square, a line. Ask them to notice any difference in energy flow during the channeling of light and love to each other. Afterwards, the activity could be describing the difference by drawing, painting or cutting and pasting the different shapes in which they meditated and sent each other love and light.

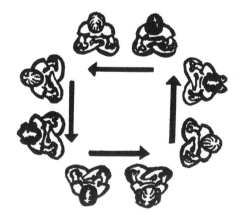
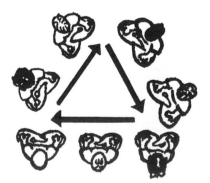

2. The Amoeba Roll — After the meditation: creative drama. Discuss first the process of growth and evolution of a cell. If possible, use a microscope with a slide of amoebas. If not possible, colored visual aids will help. Then have everyone gather in a large open space indoors or outdoors. Let's pretend we are all one group huddling together as one cell in the ocean of Being which moves like a blob and we are all part of this blob that wiggles and we move and roll in and around and through each other for a few minutes. Then when the teacher rings a bell the cell decides to divide, the amoeba splits and we all split apart into two groups. And now there is space, we have created space, there are two and there is space in between and we keep dividing each time the bell rings into 3 amoebas, and 4, etc., until we are all individuals. We have gone from Being One to many.

3. Show the children the picture of the development of the brain and the chart of evolution (see pages 144 and 145). Discuss the idea of the earth as being a big school for everyone. Ask the children what they see their parents learning in the earth school. Discuss.

4. After a number of class sessions discuss with the children ways in which meditation or going to the Source in the Center of their being can help them with their work in school and in their friendships and relationships at home. Go through a process of teaching the children what is called the method of invocation. Have them get still and centered and then ask themselves in a whisper or silently within to be open and receptive (in math class, for example) in order to learn more easily, and to send love to their teacher to help them to be more in tune with the teacher during class.

Explain how love is like a wave that goes from one person to another carrying that which is in the giver of the love's consciousness and bringing the consciousness of the giver and the receiver closer to being one consciousness. Illustrate this through dance, or a drawing, or dramatize it for the children to see clearly.

Have the children practice sending beautiful thoughts to a friend or teacher from their hearts when they want to convey something to the friend or teacher. With practice and repetition (always repeat these techniques in order to make them part of the consciousness and not just a one time experiment) children will come to understand the magic of sending love and can be asked to channel love into a difficult situation rather than getting caught up in problems themselves. If they want someone to like them who they feel does not, they can tap the power of love and send love to the person and eventually the person will either be drawn to them or they will feel satisfied that they have done their best in giving. Experiments such as this one are being carried out through psychology departments in different schools including one the author read about in Visalia, California.

An experiment can be conducted over a period of several weeks with each child noting the results of spending part of each session sending love. First sending love to someone who doesn't like them and then to another person whom they don't like and observing how the power of love can change the first person to possibly like them more and change the child to like the second person, more than they did. A discussion period with everyone participating in answering the questions, Why do people love you? Why do you love certain people? The leader can write down the answers and compile them to be reviewed and expanded upon at later sessions.

5. Use the aid of a magnet to show how love is like a magnet. When your heart is full of love it attracts other hearts to it like a magnet attracts iron filings. Using analogy, the Source within is like a magnet, a spark of Life, and when we go to the Source within we are magnetized to it and we attract more of It – more Light and more Love and more Life – both from within and without. When we give love we attract love.

6. Watch a fish in water. Imagine we are in an Ocean of Being and don't know it, just like the fish is always in water and doesn't know it because he is always in the water and never out of the water.

7. Have a battery cell and a light bulb that is 3-way. Illustrate how electricity lights up the bulb just as the Source within lights up our body with life and keeps it energized. By turning up the 3-way bulb illustrate how the bulb gets brighter – the more we can turn up the amount of light and love energy we give to ourselves and others, the brighter lights we become. Discuss what happens if too much energy comes into the light bulb, too much energy for what the light is able to handle. It breaks – this is why we develop slowly and rhythmically; this is why evolution is slow and rhythmic.

8. Use a prism to reflect sunlight. Discuss color and clear light. The Source is pure light and the mind is a prism that refracts it into color and thoughts. Study the color spectrum in order to see what different forms occur due to different rates of vibration, yet the light substance is the same. It is all vibration. Use an illustration of the spectrum in a basic physics book to show that vibration differentiates into wavelengths and we experience sound, color, etc., depending upon the different wavelengths.

9. Illustrate the nature of the mind by having a bowl of water with the sun shining on it and the sun or the source of light being clearly reflected on the water when the water is still. Then put a pebble in the water and watch the ripples. Compare this to the same process that occurs when a thought in the mind creates waves that distort the sun's reflection within the bowl. Our mind is like the water. If we can keep it calm by focussing our mind in our heart, then we won't disturb it with the pebbles of our thoughts. The light from the Source within us can light up our awareness, just as the reflection of the sunlight on still water lights up the water. Again watch the pebble create ripples in the water. See how the waves repeat themselves. See how our thoughts create other thoughts and similar ripples and waves in our minds.

10. Create steam, liquid and ice in order to see the different forms of matter from the same substance – water.

11. Study the 5 senses as receivers of vibrations of different wave lengths. Close off the ears and listen to the hum of your inside sound. That is the first vibration before all of the other vibrations that we perceive through our senses.

12. Read from different Master teachers illustrating the principles and ideas they are endeavoring to convey.

13. Play tapes of different meditations and music for inspiration.*

14. Close the eyes, press the eyelids with the fingers — see the black and white checkerboard pattern of energy.

15. Study the different Golden books or other children's books on science and draw analogies with the human experience; astronomy, the atom, the ear, the eye, etc. Relate to consciousness whenever you are able to and ask the children to relate the different functions investigated to how they work in their own consciousness. Examples are given in the class outlines.

16. Sound awareness exercise. Have everyone seated at a table with pencil and paper. Now, in the silence, write down the first 10 different sounds that you hear. What was the first sound that you remember hearing when you awoke this morning? Write this down. What was the last sound that you heard when you went to bed last night? Be aware tonight and tomorrow morning of the last and first sounds and write them down. Bring them to the next class and share them. We do this exercise to become more aware of our sense of hearing.

*Buddy Bubbles, Heart Zones and Speed of Balance cassette tapes
available from Planetary Publications (see pages 156-158).

17. Space awareness exercise. The leader sits in the center of a large circle, the children sit around on the periphery, not touching. The leader gives the signal and says – everyone come to me on your tummies, now go back on your tummies, everyone come to me on your knees and elbows, now go back on your knees and elbows, everyone come to me on your hands and tiptoes, now go back on your hands and tiptoes, everyone come to me backwards, now go back backwards, now come to me touching just one other person, and go back touching just 1 other person, now come to me touching 2 people, and now go back touching no one, feeling the space in between. Now, this time, come to me with your minds and hearts only, leave your bodies where they are. See if anyone can see the streams of energy going between us. Okay, now I am going to send your mind and heart energy back to you each one in turn. Can you feel it?

18. Water witching game. Have each child, one at a time, give 1 object of their own to another child and then the first child leaves the room. The second child hides the object and then the first child comes out. He holds out his hand to pick up the vibrations of his object through his fingers and attempts to get very quiet in the heart and to attune himself to this object and find it. He practices this attuning by holding his hand out in 3 different parts of the room in triangle form. He observes whether he picks up the vibrations in the same place. The triangle form, as well as the 3 trials, helps to focus in on the energy with greater certainty. Until practiced several times slight hints can be given, such as – you are getting closer. The child should always be encouraged to pursue until he finds the object to develop his ability to attune to vibration.

19. Telepathy. One child sits in front of another. One holds the wrists of the other. The one to receive is the one who holds the wrists and attempts to receive a thought or idea projected by the broadcaster who is having his wrists held. They then switch roles. (Both 18 and 19 were very successful with children ages 5 to 10. Interestingly, in our classes, a child was usually stronger in one or the other exercise, not equally strong in both.)

20. Scavenger hunt. Have a scavenger hunt looking for: a) objects of all the 7 colors of the spectrum, or b) samples from the mineral kingdom, the plant kingdom, the animal kingdom, etc. Then meditate on the nature of the 7 different colors or 3 different kingdoms. Try to get inside the world of the color, of the mineral or plant or animal. What does it feel like from inside?

21. Plant a garden or plant indoor plants and channel love to some plants each day and do not channel to other plants but give them all the same amount of sun and water; see the differences in the growth process. The ones that have had love channeled to them by the group of children every day should grow much more rapidly. Also discuss the process of photosynthesis. Channeling techniques given on page 113.

22. With a philodendron, have the children, one at a time, pass their hand over a leaf about 2 inches away from the leaf and tune into the energy currents of the plant. Pass the hand first across – then in an up and down pumping motion. Then have them channel love to the plant, and finally, as a group, lead them through meditation to go inside the plant and experience the life of the philodendron.

23. Sitting at a table, spread so you can't touch each other. Now, see a milk bottle in front of you in your imagination and walk right inside of it. We can imagine anything, so see your milk bottle from inside of it and from outside of it. The milk bottle is your territory now and yours alone. There is an opening at the top where you can be reached if you are needed. Now, when I make a sign with my hand you receive in your minds only what comes to you from the top of the milk bottle. You know how when you daydream you are in between sleeping and waking, in another place? Let's go to that place now so we can receive the messages better. Try to feel that space, there. . . now feel the hole of the milk bottle right above your head. Very quietly, look up inside yourself and whatever idea comes to you, let the idea flow from the top of your head through your heart and hand and out onto your paper. The ideas can be crazy or serious, poetry or prose – anything. Keep them flowing and write them down. (For little children – draw them). After the children are finished, have them share their papers with each other by reading them to the group. This same experiment can be done at another time with other media – any art or craft creation.

24. Using basic chemistry principles introduce osmosis. Relate this process to an actual experiment (easily obtainable where scientific educational tools for children are sold) and relate osmosis to energy transfer in our cells, in our subjective processes, e.g. to telepathy or picking up thoughts, feelings, and vibrations from those around us.

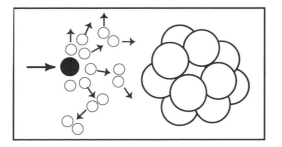

25. Stories of creation, fables, etc., to give understanding of cause and effect, to demonstrate the principles of right use of energy, are helpful to children. Have the children then make up their own stories and act them out or put them to music, etc.

26. Introduce the basic laws of gravity and radiation. Use simple physics books and experiments designed for children. Relate Newton's law of action and reaction to cause and effect in our own lives. Show how what we give out comes back to us – bad vibrations going out bring bad vibrations back; good vibrations going out bring good vibrations back. Do with meditation number 9.

27. Pendulums. Have the children each make a pendulum with a black or white string tied to a small object such as a key or a ring, or a very small ball that has a pin stuck into it so that the string may be tied around the head of the pin. A spool of black, green or white thread will also work as they are neutral colors. Provide each child with a bar magnet, or let them each take turns if there is only one bar magnet. Point the magnet north-south like a compass. (Rubbing nails against a strong magnet will magnetize the nails and each child can be given a nail magnet to place in the north-south position which is aligned with the earth's magnetic field.)

Hold the string of the pendulum between thumb and forefinger, pointing them downwards. Place the pendulum over the north pole of the magnet. After a few moments the pendulum will start to respond to the magnet's field and by itself will begin to rotate in one direction. Let it rotate for a minute or two then move your pendulum to the south pole of the magnet. After a few moments you will see the pendulum reverse its rotation to the opposite direction. Tie the pendulum to a solid object above the north pole of the magnet so you are not touching it. It doesn't rotate. Why? Because it is your consciousness interacting with the magnetic field through your nervous system that causes the rotation.

Then take a penny and, without looking to see if it is heads or tails, put it under a piece of paper. Tell your heart that if the penny is heads the pendulum will rotate clockwise, to the right, and if the penny is tails, it will rotate counterclockwise, to the left. Now, place your pendulum over the paper that the penny is under and see if the pendulum obeys your command and tells you whether the penny is heads or tails without your knowing. Don't worry if you don't always get the right answer. It takes practice!

28. Johrei is a technique of becoming a channel for healing energy from the Source through you to another object or person. A simplified version is to hold out the arm with the hand pointing upward in a relaxed state, fingers

slightly bent, and feel energy traveling from the Center within your heart down the arm and out the palm of the hand into the object or person. By channeling love and light in this manner as a group, the children can help to aid the growth of plants and animals, and can help each other feel better. If a child is hurt, it is wise to use the normal medical tools for relief plus the channeling of the healing heart energy or light. We should not experiment by relying solely on the ability of the group or any one member to heal unless the injury is very minor or solely an ego hurt.

29. One very effective and very beautiful activity-meditation to experience with the children is for all of them to channel love and light from their hearts through their hands to each child one at a time until each child feels that love energy coming into his heart and has a direct experience of the reality of consciously directed love energy. The children do this channeling while sitting in a circle and by the time each one has had a turn there is a build-up of love energy in the circle and in the whole room that is recognizable by each child and the atmosphere is usually filled with joy and peace. The whole group is made aware of the energy they have channeled and created and are now "bathing" in and as a group they send this energy to whomever they feel is in need of some of it. Whenever this experience of heart energy is occurring, the leader will find the group to be very easy to work with and the children very receptive to learning new skills. Sometimes this meditation can be followed by singing or toning. Remind the children to listen to each other as well as to themselves to create harmony and beautiful tones.

30. In conjunction with telepathy exercises in particular, discuss the brain and heart as receivers and transmitters of vibrations, thoughts and feelings. Show how we experience only part of the spectrum. Study how a walkie-talkie, radio, television or telephone work. Compare with how we receive and send ideas, feelings, thoughts via different signals to each other. Make this a creative project.

31. Nature Awareness and Trust Exercise. One child is blindfolded and leads another child around to touch leaves and twigs, rocks, flower petals, an animal, etc. This deepens sensitivity awareness.

32. Memory exercises: each child tells what he ate for breakfast or what was the first thought when he woke up in the morning and the last memory before going to sleep last night (good for all ages).

33. Presentation of materials pictorially and artistically. Young children especially tend to experience the world in pictures so all materials presented with visual aids and art speak directly to them. Art is in everything and science is in everything and art and science can be integrated in the classes as part of life instead of as isolated subjects by asking art-related and science-related questions of the children when studying any subject.

34. Spontaneous dramatizations of fairy tales with the help of props. Stories from Grimms Fairy Tales, Aesop's Fables, the Ramayana, Bible stories from different cultures are all good to introduce because all of the characters are symbolic; they are all within each one of us and the children can be asked to see themselves in each character, and not just identify with the good or bad child.

35. Action and singing games are tools for developing quick response and concentration.

36. Energy game. One person sits in a chair, four others stand by him, one by each shoulder and one by each knee. Clasp the hands and point the two forefingers out. Place the forefingers under the knee or shoulder that you are next to. Try to lift the person off the ground with just the four pairs of forefingers. Can you do it?

    Now, each of the four layer their hands above the head of the person sitting, making sure the hands don't touch each other. So we have eight hands, one on top of the other, over the head of the person in the chair. All close their eyes and imagine energy being drawn out of the top of the head into the hands. Do this with concentrated attention for about a minute. Then someone counts to 4 and on 4 everybody lifts with just the forefingers again. Watch the person leave the chair with the extra energy.

37. We each have 7 main energy centers in our body. The top of the head, the point between the eyebrows, the throat, the heart center in the middle of the chest, the solar plexus between the ribs above the stomach, the area near our belly button and the bottom of the spine. Sometimes we feel our spine ache and we have energy blocked in one of these centers. The yoga exercises are helpful for unblocking the centers. When puberty begins, the energies change and need frequent balancing. The following breathing exercise helps balance the energy and make us feel calm and relaxed.

With your thumb and little finger, gently pinch your nostrils closed. Then lift up the thumb and breathe in through that nostril to a count of 6, pinch it closed, hold for a count of 6, lift up the little finger and exhale to a count of 6, then inhale through that same nostril to a count of 6, close the little finger, hold to a count of 6, then lift up the thumb and exhale to a count of 6. Repeat 5 or 6 times slowly. Feel your self become calmer, more relaxed and more centered.

38. Musical games to promote listening. Music is a vehicle for sharing energy and exchanging vibrations. Toning different primal sounds like ahhh or ohhm creates vibrations that still the mind, making us more receptive and better able to listen.

Music ideas: chanting to different tones and simple chords, learning simple dance steps to rhythmic music. Invite individuals to play music for children to move to, or have them move to music on phonograph or tape. Make musical instruments and have the children play their own music.

Some easily made musical instruments: juice cans and boxes to make drums (paint them and attach bottle caps), small boxes, tin containers, 2 paper plates filled with beans and stapled together, gourds, bells sewn to pieces of elastic and felt, sandpaper on blocks of wood (rub 2 together), chop sticks.

39. Work with emotions, *feelings and creativity* of the children through gestalt, psycho-drama, etc. Many other awareness expanding methods used by adults can be adapted if one would simplify them for the children.

NOTE: Simple meditations and related stories written by different people are excellent and obtainable at many bookstores. Have the children practice tuning their hearts and minds to the vibration of the teacher as they listen to more fully receive the essence behind the story or meditation, just as we tune a radio exactly to get clear reception without static. Other stories from different cultures are helpful as well.

The Basic Five Steps

By now you may see a clear pattern in all these class sessions and activities.

There are really five basic steps in the Meditation Process:

1. Relaxing and releasing physical tension. We do this through yoga or energization exercises or other physical movement that emphasizes stretching and relaxing.

2. Getting in touch with the breath and releasing old feelings, then opening to new fresh positive feelings as we breathe in. We emphasize feelings of love, joy, peace, feelings that make us feel good about ourselves. Sending out heart energy always helps us to feel better.

3. Concentrating all of our energies and our mind on one central point within, focusing on a spot in the center of our heart, centering our whole awareness there to find the power of still.

4. Expanding our energies and our awareness beyond the confines of our personal egos, learning to identify with the whole, a greater life, a greater reality.

5. Grounding our energy and our expanded awareness in projects, activities, or lessons.

All of the above steps are part of developing our energy awareness and becoming a master of the energies that make us who we are. Some children will need extra help relaxing, or getting in touch, or focusing, or expanding or grounding. With children having difficulty, try to make time to lead them individually at their own pace until they are able to go at the pace of the general class. A few children may need to spend more time on Step 1 or 2 before going on to Steps 3, 4 or 5. They will greatly value this deep personal attention and contact with you. Always send love, or heart energy, to the children you work with and watch that energy come back to you in increased quality of experience.

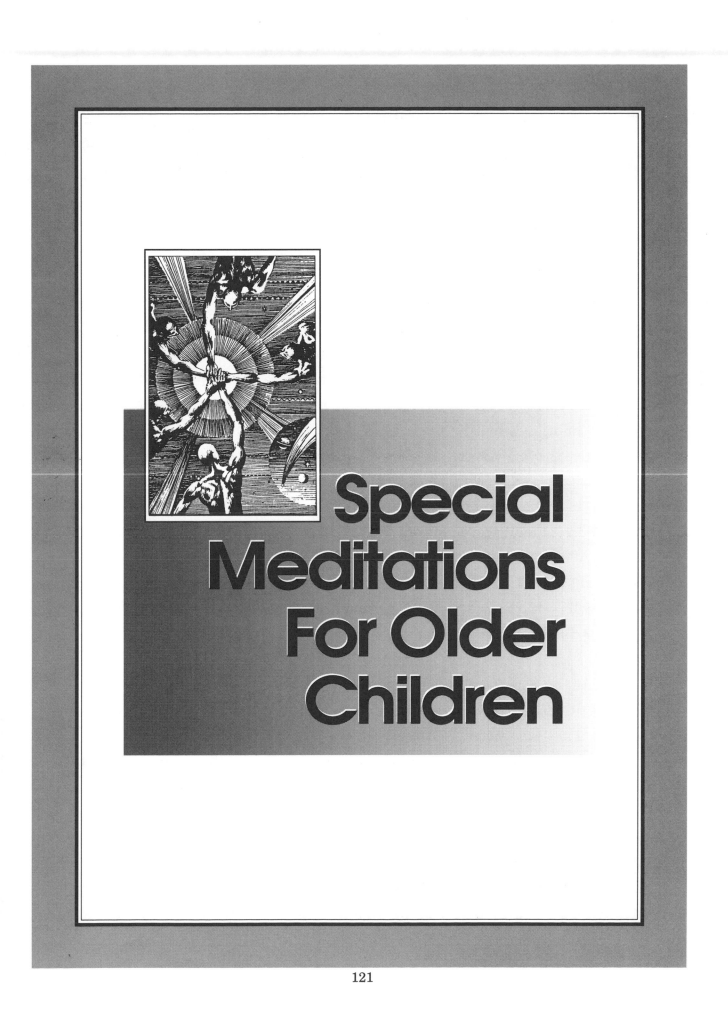

Special Meditations For Older Children

On Solving Problems

First: give the problem to the Source of wisdom within you. Surrender your worried or concerned mind to your heart which has the answer, then release the problem.

Second: ask your heart for an answer from the eternal Source of wisdom within. To ask rightly the mind has to be calm, like the moon reflected in still water, no thoughts hopping around like a monkey.

Third: wait for the answer. Sometimes it is more successful if we "sleep on the problem" because then nature gets the mind out of the way for us. Write down a solution when it comes to help you make a habit of this process. Sometimes the answer will be there for you right away, before you have even clearly defined the problem for yourself, sometimes you will need to write down all aspects of the problem, the pros and cons, just to be able to define what it really is to yourself and then your answer may appear before you or you may have to release your new clearly defined problem to the Source and wait again for the answers. Usually the first ideas that feel good to you and are good for others will be the right answer. Experiment.

Exercise: Have the children each choose something – some problem that is bothering them. Everyone goes into meditation and poses their problem silently to the Source within the heart and asks for an answer. With pen and paper write down the first positive solution that comes, no matter what it is. Also try another method – choose a problem, then describe it on paper, writing all the aspects of it down that can be thought of, listing the point of view of everyone involved, and all of the pros and cons. See if a solution is arrived at. Then take the same problem into meditation as in the first method and ask the Source. Then release the problem to the Source and forget it until an idea that feels right comes. Note it down. The next day in class, compare the answers received in the pro and con method and the answers received in the direct method. Have the children discuss what their process and experience was.

How to Apply Concentration

Use concentration techniques and develop a program to encourage concentration. Have the children each suggest incentives and methods for concentration. Synthesize these suggestions together with the children and apply the ones chosen. Discuss the principles of concentration and the effects of the methods that the children apply. As we learn to concentrate in meditation, in studying, in sports, in daily activities, all of life comes gradually into clearer focus; we acquire a better and clearer understanding of the nature of the Whole and of our relationships by the elimination of distracting and  confusing energy. Then nothing seems separate, rather all seems related. Concentration can give us an understanding of energy and how it works in us and in our environment. We gain a working understanding of the law of cause and effect and how like attracts like. We learn to see causes behind the appearances, which we come to recognize as effects. For example, through a study of astrology we can understand some causes for certain energy patterns that we see in people born under the different signs of the zodiac. This understanding can assist us in getting out of the rut of using our consciousness to judge good and bad into a place where we can observe the differences in others as different energies and where we can observe the world as it is, without coloring it with our own values. A study of Newton's Law of each action having an equal and opposite reaction can help us understand the nature of motion, whether of an atom, a molecule, or our thoughts and actions, the happenings in history or in our own lives. We can see how the biblical application of an eye for an eye and a tooth for a tooth is an extension of this law and relate events to the law – what you sow you shall reap – or the law of karma, as it is called in the East.

123

How To Apply Concentration

Exercise 1

Look back over your life. See if you can see any cause and effect patterns that have left peaceful or joyful memories.

Exercise 2

For 1 week look for and write down all examples of this law of cause and effect that you see happening around you. Be sure to include in your list examples that are caused by physical happenings, examples that are caused by emotions, and examples that are caused by thinking in a certain way. Share the results and see if you can draw some conclusions from them as a group.

Exercise 3

Concentrate on an object. Any object will do – a desk, picture, vase, etc. Observe the form of the object, the appearance . . . observe the quality of the object, is it ugly, is it appealing, is it plain, is it disturbing, etc. . . . Observe the purpose of the object, why was it created . . . e.g. a chair. The appearance is: it is made of wood and has a straight back with a molded seat and slightly curved legs. The quality is: It is simple and pleasant to look at. The slightly curved legs make it seem rather feminine as if it is grace-fully holding up the seat. The purpose is: so that someone can sit in it and be comfortable.

How To Apply Concentration

As this meditation is repeated, the student will begin to see how his values color his experience of the quality of things and events. By looking at life and other people in a similar manner, greater awareness will dawn upon the student's mind.

Exercise 4

Meditate on the intellect, the mind that analyzes . . . now shift the attention to the sense of I-ness within, that which we call I, myself. Now shift the attention to the place within where inspiration seemingly from nowhere comes. Observe these different aspects of your consciousness. Observe them and how they affect your life over the next few days and write a paper on them. Share the papers with each other (in a large classroom the class can be divided into groups to do this) and see if you can draw some conclusions as a group as to the nature of these different aspects of consciousness; then discuss the conclusions of the different groups and come to some agreements as a class.

What other aspects of consciousness are there? Can we observe how they work in us too? One or two at a time (e.g. possessiveness, jealousy, desire, etc.).

Summary: A Note To The Teacher

Experimentation with the suggestions in this book will lead to an unfolding expansion of awareness for the leader and children alike. It is best if the leader can, whenever possible, stay at least one step ahead of the children by researching the subject and practicing the meditations and exercises before the class in order to know what is being developed or exercised in the different activities. This should aid with the balanced development of the class.

Basically, the process of integrating these meditations into a school classroom has been left to the teacher. This is intentional because so many changes are now occurring in classroom policy – changes concerning age groups of children as well as change in curriculum. The meditation guidelines are flexible enough so that they should be able to be integrated into any type of class situation with slight modification. If you don't see how you can possibly integrate them into your particular situation, pick out the elements you feel you can use, keeping as much of the rhythmic patterning as possible, and leave the rest until you can see a way to use it.

The most important thing is to explore, to experiment with these guidelines and, above all else, to enjoy the fun and rewarding results.

**Teacher's Drawing
from
Meditation**

The
Applications

Personal Account

I began using meditation in the classroom the day after Deborah Rozman spoke at our school district inservice. I started the children with the simple exercise: relaxation, breathing and concentration on a star between their eyes while concentrating on having a good day and doing well in all that they were doing. I call the exercise centering and concentrating our energies. We center five minutes in the morning and ten minutes in the afternoon. If the children come in over-active from any recess, we center before beginning work. I told parents who work in my classroom as volunteers that the centering was a relaxation exercise for increasing the children's concentration. These parents accept what I am doing in a positive way and participate with us.

A wonderful thing is happening in my classroom which I feel is a direct result of meditation. I seldom have to discipline the children. They have increased in self-direction. There is a peaceful, mellow feeling or atmosphere in the room and it is a pleasure to be in the atmosphere. I feel a group awareness is evolving. The children seem closer to one another and care more for each other. They seldom fight, and if they have disagreement are often able to resolve it themselves. The "I don't like boys," or "I don't like girls" attitude, which has always been prevalent in my primary classrooms over the past seven years and which discussion could not eradicate, is disappearing through meditation. Boys and girls are interacting more. This change of consciousness is apparent but slow.

I have noticed a definite change on the playground which I attribute to meditation. Previous to meditation some of the boys in my classroom were functioning on the playground as a sort of gang, causing problems for other students. Now, without any direction from myself, most of my boys (and some of my girls) play soccer or football at recess. They taught one another how to play the games. They organize their own teams, play the games, referee the games all on their own, with a minimal amount of angry feelings. It amazes me to watch them. I never thought this age child (7-8 yrs.) could learn to interact in such a way. I watch but seldom supervise. They are proud to play in my presence.

I encourage the children to meditate on their own. Some have related

by Elementary Educator Stephanie Herzog

experiences of doing better in sports. Some have fallen asleep doing it. We need to discuss what they are practicing on their own more. I have noticed recently when we are all quiet together as a group that a nice feeling of peace comes over and into me. I have always had some problem in the classroom with keeping the children quiet while I am giving directions. Since meditation I am finding that the children are very attentive when I speak. It is so delightful! Each day flows smoothly. I also find I am beginning to speak more to the inner parts of the children.

I try to open my heart by doing the meditations and yoga every morning and lunch apart from the children as well as with them. The difference is amazing. I find that to the extent I allow myself to become uncentered, anxious or scattered, the children become anxious and noisy. They pick up my energy and send it back. I become more uncentered – and it all snowballs. Now I try to stay centered realizing I can only do so much in a day.

The meditations using the imagination, such as the balloon meditation, have been most successful. The children love them – and simply shine with energy and quiet excitement afterwards. I tell the children that we are using the same imagination that we write stories with, or paint with, except we are doing it in our minds. The children are asking to write creative stories about their experiences, so painting and writing after this type of meditation is our next step. I am glad the suggestion came from them.

One experience from meditation that was beautiful to me was in relation to a child's mother who was talking to me about some difficulty she was having with her husband. As she was expressing her concern her son walked in. He said, "Mom, the trouble with you is that you don't center yourself." She asked him to show her how which he did BEAUTIFULLY, and a wonderful communication happened then between the three of us. I had not known that the meditations had affected him so much since he had always seemed somewhat resistant to them.

I am truly committed to using *Meditating With Children* in the classroom.

Report by the Author

An excerpt from the 1977 edition:

It has only been 18 months since *Meditating With Children* first came off the press. Now in its third printing, we feel we should share some of the feedback that has come to us regarding its success. In some very significant ways the feedback has exceeded our expectations. We found that invariably when these activities were used regularly the following results occurred in the group:

- a calm vibration throughout the group
- more receptivity on the part of the children
- a sense of fellowship or community experience
- an awakening sensitivity and empathy with other people
- deeper sharing
- acceptance of feelings
- increased creative expression
- an improved self-concept
- an awakening of the imagination and parts of themselves the children had not explored.

We knew the potential was there all along for meditation and awareness activities to spark such results, but to actually experience them on a wide scale and to hear about their happening in the public school system, in homes and small groups throughout the country, is tremendous confirmation.

We deliberately chose to use the term "Meditating" in our title in spite of the knowledge that some educators and parents would react negatively to the word and associate it with religion. We feel it is important to restore the term meditation to its rightful, non-religious definition since it is based on a rich, ancient tradition of confronting our

Deborah Rozman, Ph.D.

mind and self-sense to gain expansion of awareness. Real meditation as translated directly from the Sanskrit means "doing the wisdom" and involves the wholistic integration of body, mind, feelings and internal energies, so the entire consciousness functions as a harmonious whole. No child or adult can be a complete person until he is able to stay in touch with his inner reality and be aware of its effects on his relationships with others and in his expression. What higher goal can education offer than to educate whole, integrated beings?

If you still have trouble with the word "Meditation" when bringing this program to your children, parents, family, school administrators or board of educators, use alternative terms like Stephanie does, such as awareness training, concentration, centering, awareness games, relaxation, wholistic learning, creative imagery, etc.

Report by the Author

Our greatest surprises in the feedback we have received were the reports on hyperactive children receiving great benefits from *Meditating with Children*. Hyperactivity is on the seemingly rampant increase. It has been blamed on stress, poor food, the rat race, television, permissive child-rearing, traumatic experiences and uptight parents. My own feeling is that many hyperactive children are very sensitive. They simply cannot handle the vast amount of stimuli constantly bombarding them from any or all of the above-mentioned factors. Biochemical processes that other children can handle, they react to. An emotionally upset parent that other children tune out or deal with in other ways, they take on as their own problem, quite unconsciously. The pace and demands of life, family and school environments, do not provide for the necessary conditions to deal with their sensitivities and internal energies. Through centering, deep breathing, scientific relaxation and the opportunity to get in touch with and express feelings the sensitivity is acknowledged, creatively expressed and balanced out.

DEFENSIVENESS

In the same way the child who often puts on a tough, defensive exterior, particularly in adolescence, is usually hiding a sensitive being underneath that has not been acknowledged. Again, the opportunity to get in touch with their inner feelings and needs, and have that time be socially and educationally acceptable, has softened their expressions and actions, melted the defensive exterior and brought a new mode of relating through OPENNESS.

SELF-CONCEPT

The importance of self-integration for building self-worth cannot be overlooked. It is like trying to build a bridge without all the necessary

Deborah Rozman

tools – something is bound to go wrong. Education must concern itself with self-integration otherwise we will continue to have the mounting difficulties besetting nearly every school district. With self-integration comes the ability to think for oneself and not be swayed by the need to conform to peer pressures. Rather the peer emphasis becomes one of honesty rather than conformity to rebellious acts or non-conformist antics. When personal creativity increases, the need to follow or to succumb to the herd instinct for confirmation decreases.

THE MENTALLY GIFTED

Another group we found to be most responsive to these techniques is the mentally gifted. There is a problem with challenging and motivating many mentally gifted children. Many are rejecting the idea of college, preferring life experience for their teacher. There is much discussion among educators and psychologists regarding right hemisphere/ left hemisphere brain development. It is generally agreed that the right side of the brain is not as well-educated through our school system or society, and many suggest that the right brain almost atrophies or ceases to grow much after age six. The whole dimension of meditation, creative imagery, awareness games, exercising intuition, expanding sensitivity towards others' inner worlds that is presented in this book, is a text for right brain development and for balancing the two hemispheres of the brain so that they can work and grow harmoniously together.

THE RETARDED AND HANDICAPPED

The other areas in special education (such as the retarded and handicapped) also are exploring the uses of these exercises in their curriculum. Many of the techniques are simple enough for a pre-

135

Report by the Author

schooler to begin. They bring a vital opportunity that may never be otherwise possible – for these children to awaken dormant potential through exercising awareness in games that develop non-intellective faculties. Often the children in special education are more sensitive to the right brain functions than average children, and they can grow along these lines instead.

SUMMARY

There are always some children who simply will not "take" these methods seriously immediately. They should never be forced to comply, but allowed to do some other activity during the meditation period or just remain silent while the others participate. Often these children join in of their own accord later on, or in some cases will join in the more active meditations and awareness games. When teachers can learn to perceive behavior in terms of energies – physical, emotional or mental – then the psychic energies of the group can be seen and understood in terms of receptivity, nervousness, harmony, tension, love, peace, boredom, joy, etc. Then the teacher can respond according to the need and the vibration he or she would like to create. Often children are direct mirrors for the state of consciousness of the parent, leader or teacher with whom the children are always psychically linked by virtue of the authority role the director plays.

The results you achieve with your children will be directly proportional to the frequency and duration of using these meditations and awareness techniques. It doesn't matter so much how long a time you meditate or do the activity at any one sitting, but that you do them regularly, with full attention and frequent repetition over a period of time. Even 5-10 minutes a day for "centering up" as one classroom has named it will show wonderful results which increase with time.

"THE MIRROR EFFECT"

"THE CHILDREN REFLECT UNCONSCIOUSLY THE STATE OF THE TEACHER OR PARENT"

HEARTFLOW · RADIANCE · JOY · PEACE

UPTIGHTNESS · FRUSTRATION · HYPERACTIVE · ANGER

("THE FRAZZLE EFFECT")

THE MIRROR EFFECT shows how the teacher's inner world is often mirrored by the children. Children unconsciously relate and respond to vibrations which change as you change, in direct biofeedback. Learning to stay heart centered in a state of balanced care helps teachers prevent drain or burnout.

Conclusion: The Next Step

Life mirrors back to us our inner attitude and perspective. As energy goes out, so it comes back. The mirror of life can be demanding and draining if we constantly operate from the head without input from our heart feelings and intuition. Experiment. See what life mirrors back to you when you are reacting just from the head versus when you are centered in your heart. There's a world of difference in the quality of your experience and in understanding. When you are in the head over-analyzing, worrying, judging or resenting, it's easy to become irritated, frustrated or angry. Those negative head reactions don't just go away. They accumulate in your system as negative mental and emotional attitudes, drain your energy, and release stress hormones into your body which lead to burn-out or illness. That negative energy also impacts your environment affecting those around you. By shifting to heart centeredness and putting the head in neutral, you change the quality of your energy. When you put out heart energies — love, forgiveness, compassion, appreciation and understanding — those energies also go into your system and impact your environment. Science is proving that heart energy causes different hormonal releases which are nurturing and regenerative to your entire mental, emotional and physical natures. As you practice becoming more heart centered in your interactions with children, you can see a transformation take place. Heart centeredness widens perspective and expands intuitive insight on how to handle challenging situations more peacefully and creatively. Your head and heart, thoughts and feelings, work together in a dynamic joint venture to bring more quality experiences to you.

HEARTMATH

HeartMath is a proven system to get your heart and head in sync. From my experience, it is the next step past meditation and is the future of accelerated inner growth. HeartMath gives adults and children the ability to get into the meditative state fast (heart/brain entrainment) and sustain that awareness in the midst of activity. We have been studying children who practice HeartMath tools over many years. These children show accelerated awareness, emotional balance and maturity, and high self-esteem. They are happy, well-adjusted, and do well in school. New HeartMath tools, games and techniques for parents, teachers and children are now available in the books, *A Parenting Manual: Heart Hope for the Family* and its companion guide, *Teaching Children to Love: 80 Games and Fun Activities for Raising Balanced Children in Unbalanced Times*, both by Doc Lew Childre, founder of the Institute of HeartMath. To me these books represent a quantum leap in child rearing and child development.*

A Parenting Manual: Heart Hope for the Family and its companion guide, *Teaching Children to Love: 80 Games and Fun Activities for Raising Balanced Children in Unbalanced Times*, by Doc Lew Childre, are published by Planetary Publications. Doc also wrote a book to help teenagers develop their heart smarts that I highly recommend called, *The How To Book of Teen Self-Discovery*. I was privileged to be a contributing editor in all three of these book. See page 161 to order.

Conclusion: The Next Step

Doc Lew Childre spent over twenty years researching and developing the HeartMath system. He offers a unique perspective of parents' and children's needs and the critical role the heart plays in brain function and decision-making. One of his revolutionary discoveries is that *heart intelligence* is what provides the harmonious integration of physical, mental, and emotional intelligence, leading to a more complete intelligence. Heart intelligence synchronizes the emotions and mind, bringing them into coherence and harmony. As educator Joseph Chilton Pearce states in his introduction to *Teaching Children to Love*, which I will paraphrase, "The heart is connected with the prefrontal lobes through the emotional brain, and higher heart qualities (such as compassion, real love, and intuitive understanding) are available through this connection, giving us access to a radically different form of intelligence at maturity. However, we can only access this higher intelligence if that emotional brain has itself been fully developed." While childhood and adolescence are "stage-specific" times for emotional development, most parents and teachers find it a huge challenge to emotionally guide children. Through HeartMath, adults can complete their own emotional development and have the heart intelligence and tools to wisely guide their children. HeartMath tools are now being successfully taught in the military, in corporations, schools, correctional institutions, hospitals, churches, parenting organizations and day care centers.

Young children are naturally active beings. They learn heart intelligence and basic core values through seeing adults model heart intelligence and through experiencing their own heart in action. Children often recognize and understand the difference between the head and the heart more quickly than adults. A four-year-old child who had never experienced any HeartMath training was asked by her mother who had just arrived home from a HeartMath seminar, "What's the difference between your head and your heart?" The child replied, "When I'm in my head I'm cranky and when I'm in my heart I'm happy." She knew the difference by how she felt inside.

Learning is enhanced when we feel peaceful and good inside. The expressions, "Put your heart into your work," "Go deep into your heart for an answer," "Listen to your heart," or "Follow your heart," are not just metaphorical phrases. They refer to the heart as a source of strength and potential intelligence. When we give children a solid bottom line they can stand on — the ability to go back to heart centeredness when problems arise and find new solutions — they are better able to handle stress and all the changes the world is going through with much more hope, love, wisdom, and balance.

Charts
Diagrams
Stories and
Yoga Postures

Crafts

This list of ideas can be used as activities to follow meditation. They provide creative expression to the higher energies contacted and experienced in meditation and can greatly enhance children's creativity and integration of body, mind and heart.

1. finger paint (homemade with glycerin, soap flakes, vegetable coloring, powder paint) (use glossy paper)
2. crayon drawing
3. colored felt pens drawing
4. playdough (flour, cornstarch, water, food coloring)
5. clay (use boards underneath clay)
6. paste and burlap
7. sponges for brushes
8. dried weeds, glue and cardboard
9. string painting
10. ink blots
11. block printing with any object
12. spatter painting (do outside)
13. squeeze bottle, spray, sprinkle paint
14. collages
15. nature collage on burlap
16. prints - put things under paper to get impressions, scribble with crayon
17. paper bag puppets - have a puppet show created by imagination of the children
18. batik
19. tie dye
20. macrame
21. paste colored yarn in designs on paper
22. work with different symbols and geometrical cut outs
23. show samples of mandalas, discuss principles, meditate on mandalas, have children make their own mandalas
24. paint rocks
25. needle and thread work
26. knots and braids for finger coordination
27. potato prints and crayon
28. water color

The Source

EXISTENCE • CONSCIOUSNESS • BLISS
Spirit – Selflessness – no selfness because you are all selves

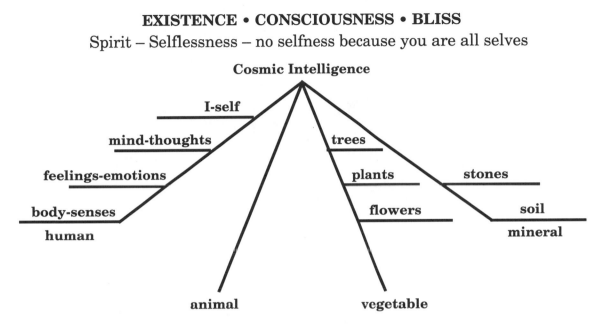

ALL IS CONSCIOUSNESS • ALL IS LIGHT • ALL IS ENERGY • ALL IS ONE

Meditation takes us back to the Source of all Life. We become one with ALL. As we learn to meditate we deepen our feelings. We deepen our thoughts. We have more energy in our bodies. We sharpen our intelligence. We become more sensitive and more aware of all life.

We wake up our brain cells and our consciousness to more life. By consciously bringing in more energy from the center, our whole self gets a bath of energy. *We experience this by learning how to:*

a) concentrate our full attention on the center

b) expand our awareness in meditation

c) exercise our bodies in a special way so the life energy can flow freely through it, and can flow freely up and down the spine and brain

d) by learning how to watch our breathing

e) by doing energy awareness exercises

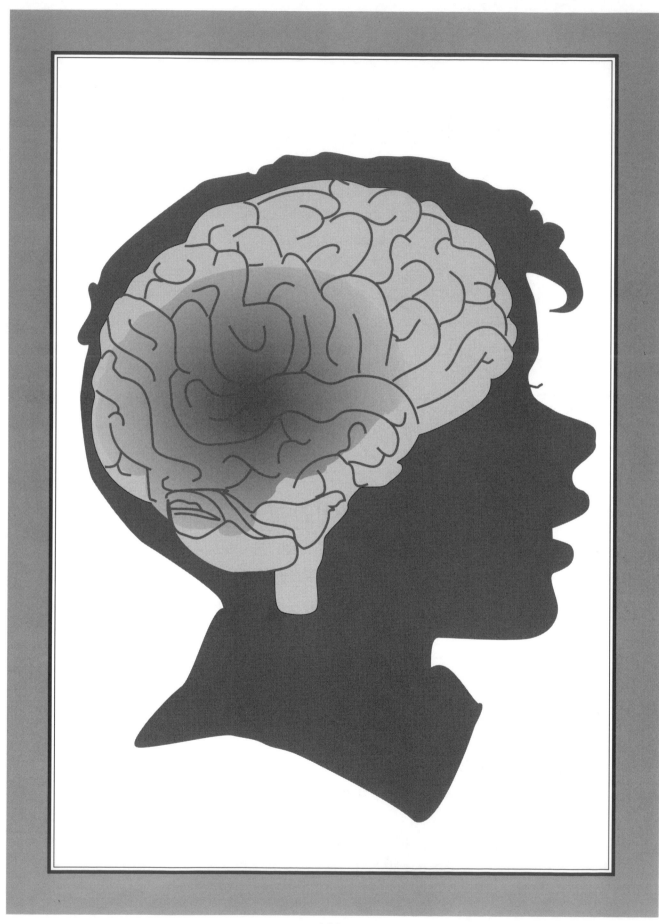

The Evolutionary Spiral

A Story: Where is the Source?

Once long ago, there lived a little boy who wanted to know where he came from before he was born. He asked his mother and he asked his grandmother and he asked his great-grandmother, who was very old, but none of them knew. Then he asked his father and his grandfather and his great-grandfather, who was even older than his great-grandmother, but they did not know either.

So the little boy sat on the stone step of his house and thought about this mystery for a long time. You know that a mystery is a thing no one understands. Well, he thought and thought and nothing happened; so he walked along the stone street and looked up at the houses and up at the sky where birds flew, but he still didn't know where it was that he came from.

At length he came to the edge of the town and walked out into the field where wild flowers grew and where white sheep and brown goats ate grass and laid down to rest. The little boy sat down once more, this time under an oak tree, and he looked up at the clouds floating far up in the heavens and he remembered that sometimes when he said his prayers at night he felt a warm softness like a feather pillow inside him and he thought perhaps that meant something.

Just then he heard a little voice which seemed to come from the grass near his feet. He looked all over but there was no one there. Then he looked up into the tree, but no one was there. He looked under the rocks. Still no one, and then the little voice spoke again. The little boy listened carefully, almost without breathing, and the voice said, "I'm inside your own heart. Why can't you see me?"

Adapted from writing **by Marvel Ulrich**

The little boy was frightened and yet excited with a thrilling joy, and he answered bravely, "Why do you hide in my heart? I can't see you there."

The little voice said, "But can't you feel me when I love you so much?"

The little boy stood up and took a deep breath. "No one can see inside himself," he said, "but I hope you'll show me what you mean tomorrow."

The little voice said, "Dear little boy, I'll show you now."

The little boy felt his eyes go back, deep within, and he saw the sun and the moon and the stars and far out in the sky   the Milky Way.

Though it was daylight, he saw all those things and the voice said, "I am all these things and I am you too. Look at them and look at everyone you love and you can see me as I see you."

Then the little boy went back to the town and down the stone street to his own house feeling like he was walking on air – he felt so light, so joyous. He told his mother about the voice in his heart and he told his father and his grandfather and his grandmother and his great-grandfather and his great-grandmother.

They all sat around the big table in their kitchen and talked about the little voice and wondered what it meant.

That night they all went to sleep in their beds and dreamed of the voice. It cried out to all of them.

"Don't you know I love you all? I live here in the heart with you and love you as I love all people I have made. Be kind and love each other as I love you so everyone will know you are my children, and will love me too."

Children's Yoga Exercise Class

YOGA POSTURES

demonstrated by 15 year old Karen

Think of yourself in a space control tower in the middle of your body universe. Let your universe expand with the in-breath of life energy and on the out-breath direct the energy to move your body into the positions shown below – like sending signals out to far off planets to change orbit.

Stay relaxed and focussed and try not to hold the breath or tense any part of the body during these exercises. Simply stretch on the out-breath. Do the postures in the order given and remember – be still, quiet and listen to fully experience the new feeling within yourself.

STANDING POSTURE
Stand upright, feet and toes together, looking straight ahead. Feel like you are balancing on ice skates.

BALANCING POSTURE
The Tree
Repeat on opposite side.
Reach up tall like a Redwood Tree.
Fix your eyes on a point on the wall in front of you in order to keep your balance.

by Malcolm Strutt

The Triangle
Repeat on opposite side. Keep legs and arms very straight.

The Dog Pose
Have you ever watched a dog or a cat stretch? Start on all fours, hands and knees on the ground. Lift your tailbone high in the air. Push your shoulders back and bring the head towards the knees.

The Forward Bend
Drop the arms and head towards the toes. Be a rag.

149

Children's Yoga Exercise Class

The Diamond Pose
Keep the back straight and take 6 deep breaths as you concentrate on a point on the wall in front of you.

BACKBENDING POSTURE
The Cobra
Keep shoulders down and back. Bring your chest up and be ready to strike like a snake.

SPINE TWISTING POSTURE
The Spiral
Repeat on other side. Push out your chest and spiral upwards like a tornado.

SPINE STRETCHING POSTURE
Head to Toe
Keep back of the legs on the ground and the spine straight. Be relaxed, like a jelly fish.

by Malcolm Strutt

INVERTED POSTURE

The Shoulderstand ➡ go over into ➡ **The Plough**

BREATHING

Normal Abdomen Breath

Watch your abdomen rise like a balloon on the in-breath and fall on the out-breath. Listen to the sound of your breath as it comes through the throat.

RELAXATION – The Corpse Pose

Pretend you are dead. Be like a cloud floating in the sky.

Come up to a sitting position and rub yourself all over with your hands as if you were having a bath of fresh air (life energy). When you can put yourself in any shape and hold the position in a relaxed way then you will be a YOGI.

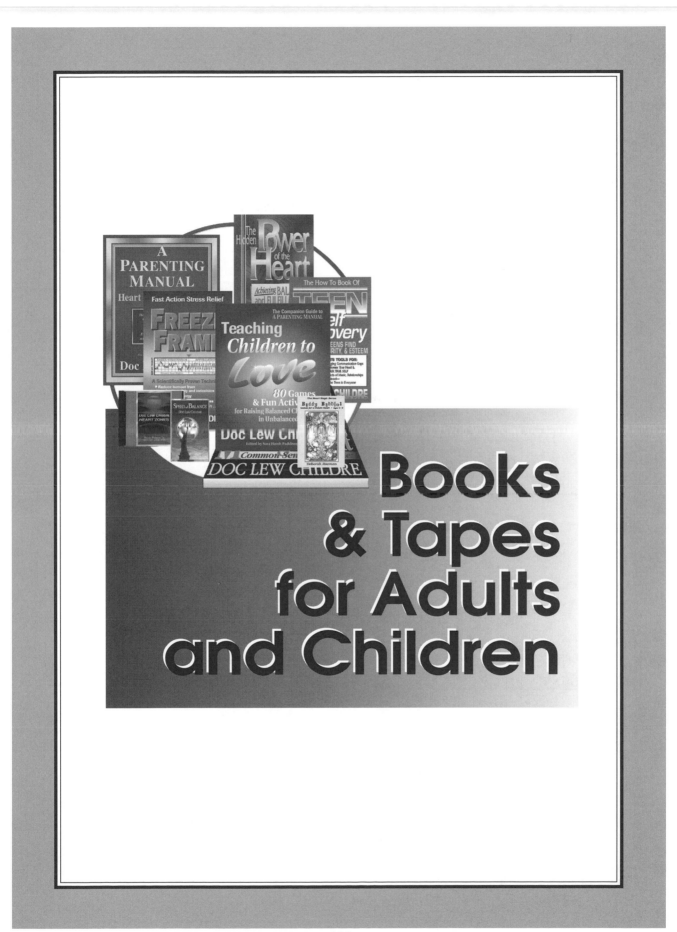

Books
& Tapes
for Adults
and Children

— AWARDED —

The National Parenting Center's Seal of Approval
for the advancement of positive parenting and effective childrearing
and selection of . . .The 1996 Read, America! Collection

THE COMPANION BOOK TO *TEACHING CHILDREN TO LOVE*

A Parenting Manual

by Doc Lew Childre

A Parenting Manual offers new, insightful information on how to parent
yourself as well as your children and provides an in-depth understanding
of the concepts that underlie the games and activities found in *Teaching
Children to Love*. Doc's intention in writing *A Parenting Manual* was to help
parents cope with their own as well as their children's stresses, strengthen
communication, and develop heart intelligence.

"A helpful, hopeful approach to the
parenting process... empowers parents by
giving them tools needed to look inside
themselves for strength and guidance."

David Katzner, President
The National Parenting Center

"...practical, down-to-earth guide in
bringing love, compassion and empathy
into all human relationships,
especially with children."

Larry Dossey, M.D., Author, Healing Words

"This is a perfect book for all parents
on this planet."

Steveanne Auerbach, Ph.D., Director
Institute for Childhood Resources

$14.95 • 152 pages • ISBN 1-879052-32-6

BASED ON THE TOOLS AND TECHNIQUES PRESENTED IN *A PARENTING MANUAL*

Teaching Children to Love

by Doc Lew Childre

Introduction by Joseph Chilton Pearce

— 80 Highly Effective Games and Activities —
A hands-on guide presented in a simple, step-by-step format
for parents, educators, childcare providers, and counselors

- Facilitates the development of positive, healthy, life skills in children
- Teaches children how to make conscious choices from the heart
- Builds self-reliance and emotional balance

The Companion Guide to
A PARENTING MANUAL

Teaching Children to Love

80 Games & Fun Activities
for Raising Balanced Children
in Unbalanced Times

Doc Lew Childre

Edited by Sara Hatch Paddison

$16.95 • 208 pages • ISBN 1-879052-26-1

For a deeper understanding of the principles presented in this book, we recommend
Doc Lew Childre's *A Parenting Manual: Heart Hope for the Family.*

The How To Book of Teen Self Discovery

Doc Lew Childre
ISBN 1-879052-36-9
$8.95 • 126 pages
Cartoon Illustrations

Find help, hope, and solutions in this book written for teens, but that talks to the teen in everyone. Offers easy tools for developing inner security and communication skills. Gives practical ways to manage emotions and reactions. Helps teens learn how to make positive choices and successfully meet the challenges of today's world.

• A *Reading Is Fundamental* approved selection
• Chosen for the 1996 *Read, America!* Collection
• Approved as a textbook by the California Department of Education

"Excellent job of introducing teenagers to their feelings — and to healthy self-esteem. An excellent tool for teenagers, adults and teachers. I recommend it highly."

— **Emmett E. Miller, M.D., California Task Force to Promote Self Esteem and Personal and Social Responsibility**

Buddy Bubbles

Deborah Rozman, Ph.D.
$9.95 • cassette tape
For ages 2-6

This lighthearted tape features delightful games, poetry, songs, and instruction to help children develop positive attitudes and self-worth. Shows children how to find warmth and security within their own heart. *Buddy Bubbles* is popular with all children and is an important resource for those who care for young children who are emotionally distraught due to life circumstances beyond their understanding. Provides a simple, heartwarming guide for children to love themselves.

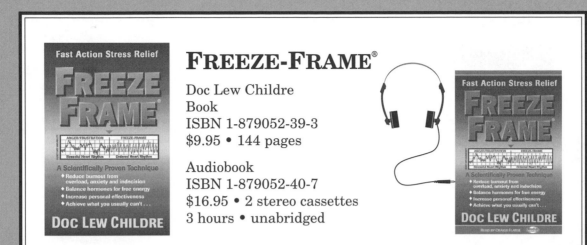

FREEZE-FRAME®

Doc Lew Childre
Book
ISBN 1-879052-39-3
$9.95 • 144 pages

Audiobook
ISBN 1-879052-40-7
$16.95 • 2 stereo cassettes
3 hours • unabridged

FREEZE-FRAME is a simple power tool for managing stress in the moment — simple enough for use in the midst of hectic family situations, by both adults and children. This scientifically-based technique is presented in both *Teaching Children to Love* and *A Parenting Manual*.

• Make lasting changes that will improve your family relationships and communication
• Manage reactive emotions like frustration and anger without repressing your feelings or losing control
• Enhance decision-making abilities
• Understand what happens in your body when you're under stress and how to change for better health and more vitality
• Increase fulfillment in family living

"If you're upset, the heart feels it. What you can do in the moment to calm yourself down is called FREEZE-FRAME."
— **Dr. Donna Willis, NBC News' *The "Today"* Show**

Heart Zones

Doc Lew Childre
Cassette $9.95
CD $15.95

Heart Zones — on *Billboard Magazine's* top sales charts for a year — is music that leaves you feeling calm, clear, and relaxed. Put it on in a traffic jam, before an important meeting, or when you just want to tune out the mind chatter. Feel focused, undisturbed, and refreshed no matter what's going on around you. Children are very responsive to the calming effects of *Heart Zones*. Specifically designed to facilitate the FREEZE-FRAME technique.

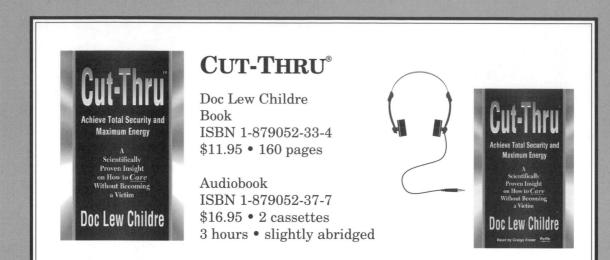

CUT-THRU®

Doc Lew Childre
Book
ISBN 1-879052-33-4
$11.95 • 160 pages

Audiobook
ISBN 1-879052-37-7
$16.95 • 2 cassettes
3 hours • slightly abridged

Learn CUT-THRU, a simple technique that shows how to turn negative emotions into peace and clarity. Feel good whenever you want to, regardless of circumstances, by discovering what this power tool can do for you. In laboratory studies measuring CUT-THRU's effectiveness, people achieved an average 100% increase in DHEA (the anti-aging hormone) — in just 30 days!

Use CUT-THRU to:
• prevent burnout
• help balance hormones and reduce PMS
• slow the aging process

"CUT-THRU explains...the crucial link between heartfelt emotions and our physical health — and then explains precisely how to apply this information in our own lives. Must reading for everyone interested in living a healthy and joy-filled life."

— **Christiane Northrup, M.D., author of *Women's Bodies, Women's Wisdom***

Speed of Balance

Doc Lew Childre
Cassette $9.95
CD $15.95

Speed of Balance creates an energizing and uplifting feeling, making it easier for you to let go of negative thoughts and emotions. Jazz enthusiasts, classical lovers, and even rock-n-rollers find it revitalizing and entertaining.

A recent research study showed that people can raise their own levels of the anti-aging hormone DHEA by practicing the CUT-THRU technique and listening to *Speed of Balance*.

The Hidden
Power of the Heart

Sara Paddison
ISBN 1-879052-35-0
$11.95 • 280 pages

This inspirational book shows how a single mother developed her heart intuition to transform her life. Sara weaves common-sense techniques into a fascinating story of triumph over insecurity and shows readers how they can do the same. Presents a profound picture of the meaning of life and the importance of bringing more love and care into daily living. Dozens of applications for bringing more fulfillment into family living.

Brief quotes from *The Hidden Power of the Heart*

• "Sincere family feelings come from the heart. They bring hope for real security and peace in this stressful world."

• "Real family is a deep feeling inside, the recognition of an inner need for support and security. Family would include the extended family, people attracted to each other based on heart resonance, and mutual support."

Women Lead With Their Hearts

A White Paper by Doc Lew Childre
$5.00 • 27 pages

Presented at the 1995 Women of Vision Conference in Washington, D.C., this brief and potent paper begins, "The empowerment of women is a global issue in the '90s." Deeply provocative, this booklet addresses the new woman of the 21st century.

Brief quotes from *Women Lead With Their Hearts*

• "When love and self-worth permeate your system, they transform fears and insecurities into self-esteem or (spirit integration)."

• Women's intuition is not just an old wives' tale. It's inner power, once women know how to access it with continuity. This increases magnetic effectiveness..."

FREEZE-FRAME®
Inner Fitness® System

Developed by Doc Lew Childre

Multimedia program includes:

- **FREEZE-FRAME Learning Guide**
- **FREEZE-FRAME Audiobook**
- **FREEZE-FRAME Book**
- **FREEZE-FRAME Video — 20 minutes**
- **Heart Zones Cassette**

Good health and well-being requires more than diet and exercise. The stress of the '90s has brought an awareness of the need for mental and emotional fitness as well. The FREEZE-FRAME Inner Fitness System provides you with everything you need to start you own "Inner Fitness" program. You will learn how to develop the mental and emotional "muscles" you need to renew your zest for life, boost your energy level, and achieve your goals. $99

Self Empowerment

Doc Lew Childre
ISBN 1-879052-34-2
$13.95 • 141 pages

A comprehensive view of today's social issues and how each individual can make a positive difference. Explains how to implement solutions to challenges everyone faces in a world of accelerating change. Doc includes wonderful anecdotes that bring his perspectives home with humor, warmth, and profound insight.

Brief quotes from *Self Empowerment*

- "The first to understand the family way of dealing with people will become examples of quality relationships within businesses, social organizations, governments and at home... sincerity in the people business is where real, lasting quality is born."

- "The earlier children understand the balance between their head and their heart, the less they will have to unlearn later in life in order to discover who they really are."

- "Care is one of our most effective outgoing energy expenditures — it is *love* in the active modality."

Institute of HeartMath
Programs and Retreats

Learn HeartMath Techniques in a Heart-Filled Environment

Come to a HeartMath Retreat in the beautiful redwood forests in the mountains of northern California. Enjoy our 150 acres of hiking trails, stunning vistas, redwood forests, and sunlit meadows. Tour the labs and music studio and explore, with our scientists, a new level of human performance. Then spend the weekend learning to listen to and access the power of your heart.

TEACHING CHILDREN TO LOVE™ — Open yourself and children to the heart of what really matters—love. It's an important and natural part of a child's fun and enjoyment in life and what's needed to raise and teach happy, balanced children. Teaching Children to Love Retreat is an opportunity to learn more about love—for yourself and the children you care for. With love, the heart imparts an intelligence that increases perception and intuitive understanding. You'll discover new perspectives and the building blocks for deeper communication, accelerated learning, self security and more love. You'll learn to create an environment in which children can feel positive and hopeful about the future. Take home simple, effective tools to help children and youth develop healthy perceptions and the mental and emotional balance they need as they meet the challenges of modern-day complexities.

HEART EMPOWERMENT® — This retreat offers an introduction to the HeartMath tools. Discover that your heart has the intelligence, wisdom and power to actualize the life you've always wanted, one with greater vitality, more creativity and more love.

WOMEN'S EMPOWERMENT™**: WOMEN LEAD WITH THEIR HEARTS** — Life has become a balancing act of responsibilities and relationships. Find solutions that bring joy and balance back into your life. Start by going where the answers really are—in your own heart.

INNER QUALITY MANAGEMENT® — Learn simple tools and techniques to achieve and sustain peak performance in the workplace by using your heart intelligence. When individuals operate at their greatest potential at work, they maximize productivity, satisfaction and quality. (Team retreats for organizations)

These three-night/two-day programs provide ample private time for learning, relaxation, recreation, and reflections. One and two-day programs can also be brought to your organization. For information about IHM programs, retreats and IHM training programs, contact:

INSTITUTE OF HEARTMATH
14700 West Park Avenue, Boulder Creek, California 95006
(408) 338-8700 fax (408) 338-9861
e-mail: hrtmath@netcom.com • http://www.webcom.com/hrtmath